BEASTS OF PREY

Beasts of Prey

The Hard Truth about Men

Orna Gadish, M.Sc.

Requests for permission should be addressed to author via email: orpub1000@gmail.com

ISBN-13: 978-1530264131

ISBN-10: 1530264138

Library of Congress Cataloging-in-Publishing data:

Gadish, Orna
Beasts of Prey. The Hard Truth about Men.

ISBN 1530264138

Manufactured in the U.S.A.

This book is based on author's research and real life experiences. For privacy reasons names have been altered except for contributing experts. The pronouns he/she and his/her are sometimes used interchangeably. The information contained herein is not designed to be a substitute for expert assistance, consultation with a therapist or mental health professional, legal or financial advice.

CONTENTS

1

Beasts of Prey

MEN & THEIR NATURAL SELECTION

I asked a male friend of mine what it is that guys look for when they go out on their first date. He took no more than five seconds to answer: buttocks. Albeit, he said it with an impish smile on his face. As clear as a blue sky: men and their libido are intimately linked. And men are so wedded to their sexual instincts that they can hardly think clearly when they see a woman, especially a good looking woman, in front of their eyes. It happens to me all the time when I start a conversation with a new guy at work. Speaking on the phone, the conversation usually flows smoothly. At times, it can even make sense. But later, say, if we need to clarify things through a face to face interaction, it usually turns into a disaster. Everything changes for the worse. So from a male perspective, I quickly go from a project manager into an object manager, or a sexual object manager, to be precise.

Research suggests that men get much "thicker" on thinking tasks after they talk to a woman—a thing that does not happen to women. Women's ability to perform on cognitive tasks after talking to a man was not compromised. The same research found that men, single or not, consider their interactions with women in terms of a "mating game." Or, as the researchers put it, "Men are prone to engage in effortful and cognitively demanding attempts to impress an opposite-sex partner."[1] Translation? Men will always try to get women laid, and that obsession takes much of their brain capacity. It does not really matter if they're married or not, if they're twenty-seven or sixty-seven, if they are at work, in the gym, or walking their dog out in the park—they will always try to impress women with their "Ferraris" first, and it doesn't really matter if they actually own a Ferrari.

The hard fact is, by nature all males are the same—hunters, beasts of prey, testosterone manipulated creatures that smell females' pheromones from a distance.[2] They will do just about anything to catch their prey and get women laid, and the sooner they do it, the better. Similarly to other males in nature, men's natural inclination is to spread their genes on planet earth through various copulations with females. And their biological target is to do it as often as they can. And, yes they can! No religious belief, no tradition, no social conventions, no ethics and morality constrains, and no legal obligations can bind that inclination down, and whoever says otherwise is probably a hypocrite or lying. The concept of "man" and the concept of "marriage" simply don't cook together.

That is not to say that the concept "man" and the concept "marriage do not overlap occasionally today for the mere sake of the legal contract of marriage.

Unfortunately, they still do, but clearly with less enthusiasm and fewer expectations from marriage than in the past.

The patriarchal marriage still happens today for the most part due to old-fashioned heritage and tradition reasons, cultural brainwashing, social pressure, political and economic interests, or government and state dictates. The patriarchal interests, politics, and money issues still govern and manipulate the institution of marriage today. Such interests make us believe that marriage is the ultimate arrangement on earth for monogamous and heterosexual relationships.

That is untrue, of course, looking at it from a political, social and cultural perspective. But first, from a biological or natural perspective, one should look closer at the dissonance between "marriage" and "mankind" to see how marriage became unnatural, artificial, and essentially useless to men.

According to the "sexual selection" theory initially put in place by Charles Darwin, reproduction with a variety of females is part of a strong survival urge to spread genes[3], and no male in the world, including members of the human species, can act against it. This primal urge is embedded within men's DNAs, whether they want it or not.

That does not take away from the fact that the human species are the highest ranking creatures on the pyramid of survival in the nature. Indeed, man is the most developed creature on our planet when it comes to intelligence, cognitive capacities such as memory, language, and learning skills, both abstract and concrete rationalization, and real life survival tactics. But when it comes to sex and relationships, partnerships, and marriages, modern men are as primitive as Bonobo monkeys. Most modern men screw up as partners for marriage and long-term relationships because they are afraid of obligations. They are scared to be bound to just one woman and hooked up with her in the marriage cell for good. No matter how old they are, where they live, and what they do for a living, all they are after is one thing. It is called SEX. But the sexual conquest is always achieved through game and excitement for men, as men really are, in a perpetual state of foreplay.

But What If He Loves Me?

Forget about love. Love is a humankind invention. It's nothing but an instinctive bio-chemical reaction to a complete STRANGER you happen to meet, a response to pheromones and sex hormones, such as testosterone and estrogen. In the attraction stage the neurotransmitters adrenaline, dopamine and serotonin play a key role, with increased stress-response levels (adrenaline), intense flow of energy, desire, and rush of pleasure (dopamine) and decreased sense of "stability" (serotonin). Later, in the attachment stage, oxytocin that is released in an orgasm is known to deepen the "bonding" between the sides, and vasopressin is believed to trick the brain to want more of this "bonding."[4]

When this attraction mechanism culminates in sex, it triggers the emotions further and deceives the woman into feeling "in love", at least for the time being. But such emotional components are a big lie. You are not "in love". Believe me. It's most certain an infatuation that is contingent and very short lived. Yet, it's undeniable that at the beginning that chemical reaction can make the man tick and attract to you like a magnet, at least for a while.

Indeed, research shows that a human male's "love" for his female partner can hold quite well for the first years[5], after which his satisfaction usually declines due to emotional and motivational erosion, which are, of course, the golden path to separation and divorce at a later stage. Apparently, marriage cannot ground men for longer periods of friendship, because when men think they own their sex exactly like a property and get used to it as well, they start taking it for granted. And it doesn't really matter if they are in a short relationship, already husbands with five kids, or if they are conductors or doctors. A short while after men get used to the same female partner, their interest in her gradually dwindles in favor of new females. At that point, again, they become game for a new prowl exactly like male beasts in nature.

Despite what we've been told in our culture about marriage as the centerpiece of modern civilization, the key to a loving family, the cause of perfect harmony, and the ultimate blessing—the true nature of men is in irreconcilable contradiction to such ideas.

Your man cares a fig about your marriage contract or your kids' failing grades at school after a new chick at the gym has turned his head (and surely his member) upside down and inside out. At that point, his testosterone and adrenaline hormones of competition and excitement have reached peak levels, and he can no longer think coherently like a civilized man.

Fortunately, most women are reasonable creatures and can take a close look at how men behave when they're around other women. All along the way women get clues that their men are interested elsewhere. And in today's world fast paced lifestyles and high speed technology do not mitigate such issues. On the contrary, real life shows us that nothing today can really glue a male to the same female partner for any lengthy period of time—no matter how pretty, smart, or sexy she is. It has nothing to do with her smile, looks, brains, or even emotions. Men's innermost natural inclination is to be driven by sex, and the environmental circumstances of the postmodern lifestyles complement this inclination.

Consider the following example. My friend, Michelle, told me recently that her three-and-a-half months old relationship with her boyfriend who broke her heart ended abruptly because she refused to become a hot busty blond like he wanted her to, that is, augment her breasts, dye her hair, and do this trendy blood red manicure and pedicure. "What an awkward line of thought," I told her. "His behavior has nothing to do with the way you look or dress, my dear." It's just that all males are short story readers, and all they want is to get to the last page, the one about sex. Inspired by their hormones and instincts, they quickly go about turning the pages, until they reach their ultimate goal. And after they get what they want and get used to it as well, they usually lose interest and need to be triggered again by another short story, another woman, and another subject of prey. In this regard, one can't expect from men any logical explanation or rationalization of their deeds, as men's hormones are their "commanders in chief," not their intellect. And so the naked truth is that notwithstanding any social convention and morality or ethical concerns—no formal agreement or marriage contract can negate this natural inclination in men to experiment with new sexual partners whenever and wherever they can.

True, our discussion here concerns essentially normative men who abide the law and not whackos, sex maniacs, or predators of any kind. True, men are usually known for their logical skills, and throughout history have become renowned thinkers, intellectuals, inventors, scientists, philosophers, engineers, writers, actors, painters, sportsmen, and political leaders, to name a few.

Yet, when it comes to relationships and long-term commitments, the vast majority of men screw up big time. The reason, first and foremost, has to do with men's biology. Men just can't act against their innermost biological nature. They have been "programmed" to physically and mentally fail to hang on in lengthy relationships, because serious relationships suffocate them. And, if they feel trapped, they will always try to escape, to look around and hunt new prey, as the hunting process itself is what turns them on, not less than the sexual pleasure.

Males will always strive to catch new females, no matter if they're in a relationship or not, because new females excite them and boost their masculine egos to new heights. Men have been competitive and mighty hunters from time immemorial. But ever since technology freed men of the kind of hunting that involved shooting wild game or tracking down enemies who physically infringed on their domains, they began to focus on closely related shooting games with women and with other possessions such as cars and different gadgets. But, unlike cars, gadgets, and other material possessions that excite men, there is nothing like a beautiful woman to spin their heads, simply because of the raise in cortisol, hormone associated with stress, which signals to men there might be an "opportunity for courtship."[6]; a thing that is incomparable to their relationships with their cars, their gadgets, or other material possessions. Undoubtedly, having such creatures marry would be an erroneous act, especially given our postmodern era; an era in which political and economic interests underlie even the most basic and naïve occurrences in life and the macro-narratives, or big stories, which are told about them in society and culture[7].

Everything is tendentious in our postmodern world, and that includes marriage. No longer can we trust any ideology conveyed to us though the media, the Internet, the papers, the radio, the TV, our academic institution, the corporation we work for, or even our own business, our community, and our family, our man or our child at home. It's all about individualism, hedonism, and interests. And patriarchal interests, that is interests originating from the side of powerful men in society and culture is the heart of the matter. We shall see a world of domination and manipulation, a world of competition and aggression, a world of double standards and lies, a universe of tyrannical suppression and exploitation of the female sex—from the past centuries up to our current time. But if there is a place to start from, it is definitely men's natural inclination, the basic attraction of men to ephemeral sex.

The biology and the behavior of males in nature, including human males, spell it out for us time and again. And the instant gratification component of our lifestyles only confirms it with a big rubber stamp.

Men are unreliable with regard to persistence in long-term relationships, with regard to "loving" the same woman, and later, with regard to investing time and energy in raising their kids. No evaluation system can ever express how bad men are in relationships, because their grade is lower than the lowest grade. Trusting one man for life would be like putting all your eggs in one basket—a colossal error, a big mistake. You must, therefore, keep yourself independent and self-sufficient at all times and also free yourself from any kind of crippling agreements or legal contracts. Such contracts are still regulated my men's interests, the institution of marriage, the government and the states.

The marriage contract should therefore be out of the question for every postmodern woman today. Even if she wants to have a boyfriend, a lover, a partner, or a father for her child, she should never concede to stale patriarchal values and life in a nuclear familial cell. A cell where the man is still the head of the family, the primary breadwinner and the decision maker of the house, and the woman still serves as the primary homemaker and child caretaker. A family where the woman should yield to the man, be suppressed by him or dependent on him physically, emotionally, or financially.

You should not allow it to happen to you. Not in full and not in part. A postmodern woman today should not surrender even a portion of her autonomy to a man—not even when the man or the society makes her believe that her compromise will be for the sake of their "perfect family." The family is not so perfect. Actually it has been idealized, romanticized, and glamorized by the patriarchal institutions and immersed in much interest, prejudice, and lie. The marital vow "To love and to cherish until death do us part" became ridiculous, because it cannot hold true in the twenty-first century. Marrying a guy in our times is a gross mistake.

There are other alternatives to living with a guy a woman cares a lot about. For instance she can "live together apart" and maintain separate households and economies. But a woman should strive to be physically, emotionally, and, above all, financially independent of her man.

The man should not know exactly what she possesses and how much money she or her family have at the start of the relationship in order to avoid unwanted strings attached. Never should a woman give the man the feeling that her fate is completely in his hands. Rather, she should stand on her own feet and establish a relationship where both of the partners are equal contributors.

Remember, in our world there's no place for the legal marriage contract. There are many reasons for that, but the first reason is the biological nature of men and their social and environmental inclination to have sex with many women outside their agreements, whenever and wherever they can. Parallel to that, there is a considerable number of women, that is sexually liberated women, who are free to compete against men in the world, and, yes, also have sex free and without inhibitions. There are plenty of casual opportunities today to have sex and create friendships, and companionships, flings, or long-term affairs. So for most men the sexual game now is "mix and match" women as they mix and match their pants, shirts, ties, and shoes.

Like products, most women today are well groomed. They are carefully made up, well-dressed, smell good, and look attractive, at least on the outside. Modern science and technology, along with the progress of the beauty industry, have allowed for this trend to happen.

This is exactly why most married men double cross their wives. The marriage contract is outdated and irrelevant to their trendy and dynamic lifestyles. In the past, lifestyles were slower paced with less exposure to beautiful women outside home. Today is a different story. Many women look much younger than their biological age, thanks to cosmetics, facial treatments, and plastic surgeries. Many women also look more beautiful and attractive to men than they naturally are thanks to the makeup, the hair, and the fashion industries. And men are surrounded by women all the time. Many of those women are young, beautiful, well educated, smart, ambitious, and can also compete with men on equal grounds. This has certainly increased the level of friction between the genders and the accessibility to free sex away from home. Naturally, men are the first to take advantage of this situation. For them, experimentation with sex is the most exciting adventure on earth, beating out any other obligations, including the marriage contract.

If, in the past, the marriage commitment was

reinforced by interests such as perseverance of family wealth, financial dependence of the woman on the man, and the need to reproduce for patriarchal inheritance, today such reasons are less dominant. Great sex and "true friendship" have become the lead factors for a relationship's success[8] (a short-lived success, though). But, the traditional marriage contract still persists thanks to religion, tradition, political and economic interests, and an inability to think outside the box. At the same time, the marriage contract is slowly but surely dying out today. And something should absolutely happen so we acknowledge that fact and say it out loud.

The traditional institution of marriage just can't answer the need of the hour. No longer can marriage be a prerequisite for anything. Not for chasing women's dreams. Not for women's independence. Not for women's success as individuals in the world. Not for academic achievement. Not for career success. Not for financial prosperity. And not even for social success with family or friends. And if family is what women are after, then no longer should marriage be a prerequisite for cohabitation or building a family nest. Not for having and raising kids. And not for "living happily ever after" with their partner or friend. The idealized concept of marriage can easily turn into a nightmare, as it turns out to be for every second couple that divorces today in the US and the western world.[9] For women living in our age, the best way to avoid a nightmare would be to shun a marriage that has a disastrous potential to smother a woman's ambitions and suffocate her dreams.

WHY MEN COMMIT

Men are mighty hunters when it comes to tracking down, pursuing, and finally shooting their prey with weapons. They are always on the prowl for women to satisfy their libido with. In men's minds, women are laid out exactly like maps. Each new encounter with a woman is nothing but an opportunity to survey that woman and estimate their chances of satisfying their primordial urge with her.

Yet, despite this natural predisposition, males frequently commit to women and tie the knot with them. What is it that confines them and makes them think of marriage despite their natural inclination and the availability of a host of potential sexual mates? It is religious influences? Conservative values? Cultural brainwashing in their heads? Social pressure? Effect of media? Because it's the right thing to do? Because everybody marries? For the sake of the kids? For the sake of Jesus and Mary? Please.

Today, there are plenty of alternatives to establish

an honest relationship based on mutual respect and sex with a man without committing to marriage; but some women are oblivious to them. They just go with the flow and don't ask the necessary questions. For instance what if he breaks the agreement on no-fault after sleeping with a "bitch" from his office and then leaves you? What about your pain as you break up? What about the jealousy? What if he's a slacker and only wants to exploit you through marriage? What if he has a bad credit history and is immersed in debts head to toe when he enters marriage? What if he spends your marital money like an idiot on his things while you are legally bound? What if he demands from you to answer his needs time and again and you really hate it? What if he threatens you to get what he wants; physically, financially, or mentally? What if he extorts you and leaves you ruined afterwards? In the past, discussion of marriage has been such a colossal taboo that nobody really questioned why in the world they need it as a necessary step to the coveted dream of family and children. But the truth of the matter is that a woman today no longer needs to marry a guy in order to establish a friendly relationship based great communication, humor, mutual trust, sex, or even to have a family with kids.

The discrepancy between the old-fashioned values and norms of marriage and the postmodern world's abundance of alternatives, both physical and symbolic, in the instant gratification super highway of our time—is exactly the problem. And when it comes to the biological predisposition of men and their natural selection of sex, the availability of potential sexual mates begging for satisfaction supports their beastly inclination. That is, the availability of sexually liberal women and their readiness to have sex with men plays in concert with men's sexual drives way more than with the puritanical values of patriarchal marriage.

Of course men would cheat on their wives. Of course they would lie to them time and again and threaten their families' stability and health when there are so many sexually available women single or married outside the home, in their office, or on their computers, just craving intercourse.

Fact is that times have changed. Relationships have become fragmented, imaginary, and virtual way more than real. In our postmodern time, contingencies and an endless variety of options to communicate, intermingle, and also mate became a living reality. Lengthy commitments became history. Males are not bound to the same physical space any more. They are constantly on the go, on the fly and can try their hand virtually anywhere, from the office to the globe, through their computers, i-Phone, and i-Pads. For instance, a man at his desk in New York can flirt virtually with a woman from San Francisco. Two days later, that same man might find a business reason to head west, get clearance from his boss, and meet his virtual find at an undisclosed location in the middle. Welcome to the digital age! Among many factors, modern technology has been a key one in bringing on this change. But rather than ignoring it, let's be wise and acknowledge that. The ideal of marriage to a large extent has lost its ground as a powerful pillar of modern society and stability. The society is no longer stable. In fact, it is shaky. Perhaps it's also more natural, contingent, variable, and creative this way, because people change and relationships change constantly. In our digital age, more and more couples get divorced, because marriage can no longer be the ultimate answer.

Nonetheless, some people still live according to the old-fashioned standards, these of their parents, their grand parents, and their great-grandparents. They think they are doing the "right thing"—that is what their social circles, community and friends would expect them to do, despite the evident changes to our society and culture across time and the advent of the postmodern generation. "You turned thirty-one and you're still unmarried? My goodness, there might be something wrong with you," your grandmother might say. Go ahead—pick your prince on the white horse, and lift your finger up in the air so he can put his thirty thousand dollar diamond ring on it. Half a year later, you'll find yourself pregnant, and you will live happily ever after. This naive American dream is already dead. The need of the hour is to revise these stale traditional norms and reinterpret them to meet the lifestyles of our postmodern civilization so that there would be no need for breaking commitments and divorcing painfully when marriages fall apart.

WHAT MEN REALLY WANT

As a species, human beings have come to understand that sex is one of the most precious components in a good relationship. We value the role that sex plays in our lives and cherish those tender moments we spend acting out our feelings for each other.

For most of the independent and usually successful women I interviewed for the book, it turns out that sex is a tender way of sharing their emotions with men. The approach is best kept slow, elegant, and classy. Such women usually like to wait to sleep with a man until they feel that a particular man deserves their passion. It's not that these women are shy or have hang-ups with sex. It's just that when it comes to the issue of female libido, they like it nice and slow first and later beat it up to a wild crescendo. That is "sexy" mixed with "classy," and perhaps that's why these women referred to sex mostly as "making love."

But males' biological setting is a lot different. For them, sex is the most coveted ultimate-prize of a sweeping conquest. It is a proof of their virility, and they are not afraid to show it off. They would drop subtle, but extremely thick, hints all the way till they gain access to that secret haven. And most men start this process quite early, during the first date.

If a guy is complimenting your dress, he is probably visualizing how soon he would rip it off your body and get his hands on you. If he says he enjoys your company, he probably means he'll want more of it a little later, in bed. Expensive gifts? Another tacky method to buy women off. The flashy Porsche and his redecorated loft in downtown Manhattan are like a chariot where he drives his prize to "his place" for an after-dinner romp. The generous smiles, the rugged features, the slight hint of stubble that most women adore, the six pack abs he's been working on day and night in the gym, the trendy clothes, and all those techie gadgets are just weapons in his colossal arsenal of seduction. There are more of them: Did you find the way he held your chair back for you, a gentlemanly gesture? Well, let's just say he wanted to take a better look at your derrière… The saddest part is that most women fall for those classical male traps only to realize later and regret that it has been just goddamn sex they were after, nothing more.

For men, the need for sex is just a buildup of biological pressure, namely real white sperm, as much as emotional pressure that they experience continually day and night.[10] From time to time, they must absolutely give vent to this buildup of pressure literally under their belt. But, hey, whoever made them think that women have to forever play the role of giving them whatever they want the moment they want it was mistaken. Again, it's the patriarchal institution's manipulations, political causes, social and cultural dictatorships, and also the old-fashioned norms and traditional stereotypes that make them think they are entitled to get whatever they want from the women.

When it comes to sex, the problem is that before the sexual act men don't think too clearly, they just act. But after the sexual act they are kings. Research proved that while men are so dense before sex, women are quite the opposite—razor sharp. But after having sex, it all turns upside down.[11] Once the males' pressure has been released, and they're disarmed of their destructive weapons, theoretically and practically they can disappear from the women's frame until the pressure builds up again. Then they will be ready to prowl again for the next partner. Sex is thus a routine test of the males' passion and not an expression of "love" of any kind as the institution of marriage makes you believe.

Heaven forbid, did I say "love"? Pardon me, my dear sister. Try to take it metaphorically and symbolically, not literally, please. Love is a widespread misconception. It populates the fairy tales, at best. It's nothing but a bio-chemical reaction to a complete stranger, a hormone manipulated deception of our brains to make us want to have sex with men and reproduce joyfully. Why would we, were it not for passion and pleasure? How else would nature or god convince us to mate?

But while men are programmed mostly for sex, women are programmed differently. For women, sex is important but they certainly don't "fall in love" through sex like men do. Most often, women would like men to stay with them for a while after intercourse and they develop an emotional attachment to men due to oxytocin, the "cuddle hormone" released after sex. But men, for the most part, view sex practically and mechanically and don't attach emotionally to the women as the women attach to the men.[12]

For these biological, psychological, and culture-change related reasons of our postmodern generation, among others, the new wave of postmodern woman would never commit to a man. The natural inclination of men to look around for prey, track new excitements all the time, and also find them immediately at their vicinity or at a click of a button on the screen has made the marriage institution hopelessly irrelevant and unsteady nowadays. As well, patriarchal marriage can no longer hold in such a fast paced, emancipated environment, where women have equated decision-making powers and authorities, as men.

In the current equal gender powers situation we face, a better alternative to traditional marriage must emerge. But the problem is that the old-fashioned contract of marriage still exists, which makes some women make the wrong decision, marry and suffer for years to come.

Clearly, the old-fashioned traditions and institutions are still lagging behind the new social and cultural roles women assume today, as well as behind the new technological settings. Above all, the institution of marriage is oblivious to the fact that men will always look for sexual variety in their surroundings as part of their biological play.

Case in point: Lauren, my neighbor and friend, recently shared her dating experience with me. She was dating this handsome six-footer whom she "loved" madly for two-and-a-half years, after which he abruptly dumped her because he thought she was flirting with another guy in an online chat. He read one message on her laptop, and suddenly everything was clear to him. She was having an affair in front of his eyes! Well, of course that was not the case for Lauren, who has been an image of honesty with the guy. It was just that her laptop from work was used by another woman who forgot to log off her online account, and it was she who was having the "sinful fling." You can call it the miracles of technology. Of course Lauren's explanation did not convince the guy, and he opted out of the game like a wicker man running from fire. But, in reality, what spoiled it was the fact her guy just didn't want to get hitched. Surprising? Not at all. What happened was that as he saw she was getting more "serious" about their relationship, he quickly lost his interest in her and looked for an excuse to split up. The moment this excuse arrived he jumped at the opportunity like he'd found a treasure. Did he stop loving her? Of course not. He probably didn't love her in the first place. He was just after sex with her. Conclusion? Men and marriage just don't double-click in our digital world, but men and sex very much do.

ANTI-CLIMAX: THE AFTERMATH OF SEX

If you met a new guy and had a few successful dates with him, it is virtually impossible to predict beforehand what his post-sex reaction would be. But one thing is sure, if it was sex he was after, he would leave the stage right after he performed his sex act and got the applause from his male friends. Often his attitude for the woman would change dramatically and drastically immediately after the intercourse. This isn't hard to notice. His interest in the woman would dwindle considerably after their hot and passionate night together, and chances are the woman would see less and less of his lovely image from then on.

Don't be disappointed if it happens to you. The disappearing act after sex has been the subject of research for evolutionary biologists. As mentioned before, for most men, sex is nothing but a conquest or a mating game. All they want is to prove to themselves and to you, weird as it sounds, that they can catch you. Once they have you, it is game over for them. They can now move on to their next conquest. Here the hunt will start again. They will search around for irresistible prey; the very chase will turn their erect apparatuses on. After they get the kill, they'll quickly come home and eat it hungrily, and later, also tell their friends how exciting it was to chase you down until you were shot and how tasty you were, heaven.

Most women explain men's strange behavior on grounds of "fear of commitment." But beyond the fear of commitment, men are also not "programmed to commit" biologically. Socially, men are also reluctant to give up on the abundance of opportunities for sex around them. They just love to maintain that fever and rush every time they are after a new prey. It is the same feeling they feel down their pants when a woman tells them how attractive they are, how smart, or how amazing they've been in bed the other night. And not that all of them are Casanovas or the greatest maestros in bed. The opposite might actually be the truth. But the typical male wants more and more of this chase and thrill. And to keep it coming and going they just move on from one conquest to the next, exactly like beasts of prey. They are not afraid of getting hooked for good. They're just scared as hell of missing the chase.

EVERYTHING BUT WEDDING

Can you explain this stupid behavior of women who agree on giving men sex right off the bat, starting from the very first date after meeting the guy and ending in years of miserable cohabitation and subordination to their rule? Psychologists' excuse for this behavior is called "separation anxiety."[13] Some women are afraid that men would lose interest in them if they decline their sex whims, so these women concede and give it to them too soon and whenever they want it. Unfortunately, some women are afraid to lose the guy because they're dependent on him financially or emotionally. That should never happen to you. You must be in full control of your body and your mind, as much as you are of your possessions and finances.

But if you've already made the mistake and got married, it does not mean he should enslave you. This is another problem with the marriage agreement. Men still see it as a sex agreement and agreement of subordination to their biological needs and their needs for homemaker and caretaker. This is the old-fashioned outlook of course. But that should not be the case for you any longer. You're a part of the postmodern society in the global age. You're not his personal property or his personal whore whatsoever, not his maid, not his cook, and not his taxi driver for the kids if you have any. So if it's only sex that keeps you together or one of the traditional gender roles that women were expected to provide to their men in the past centuries—you must definitely rewrite the rules.

But if it's more than sex, say, if you met a guy and you have been together for a while, at some point the question of marriage might pop up. In such a case, try to put the social pressure, all traditions and old-fashioned rules aside, and focus on your life. Do you really believe marrying a creature who is primary driven by his hormones and sexual instincts would be a good idea? What if you catch him looking for prey after you have taken your vows and walked down the aisle? Most often this is the case and it quickly ends up in divorce. You may consider partnership with the guy, living together, or running separate households, later even raising kids, but marriage? Oh no. That should absolutely be out of question.

So the first reason to decline marriage is the male's primordial evolutionary inclination toward sexual misconduct coupled by liberated surroundings of the digital age. But there are plenty of other reasons why a woman should not consider a marriage contract today. The first thing to keep in mind, though, is this male "natural programming." The leading driving factor in a males' mating ritual is to spread their genes on the face of earth. It might sound uprightly blunt but believe me—men are not after anything even remotely close to conjugal harmony. Not only are they childish at times, they are also more competitive, and aggressive than women and their authoritative control of sex, women, and society at large—all start from this "sexual programming" toward plentiful copulations with women and ephemeral sex.

Remember that while females look for quality in their mating rituals, males are after quantity. The greater the number of mates males lay, the better their chances of spreading their genes. And that exactly is why males feel that swell feeling under their belt each time there is a prospect of catching a new sexual partner, even though they might be married for several years, have rocking sex lives, and even have lovely kids. It's just the way they are programmed, and we can't change it for better or for worse.

Hence, a woman should never be submissive or too soft with her guy. She always needs to value her independence, gained though years of struggle and war by women liberation movements and feministic activists—and never give herself up completely to a man; not even after the man has matched up to her high standards of a classy behavior. But even if he was on his best behavior, a woman must steer clear of anything that sounds like marriage after a series of long dates or even after living together.

A man may persuade the woman by being really sweet and taking her to meet his mother in Venice. He may act like a real gentlemen, true nobleman, or be kind and honest with her. He might even send her flowers, invite her for dinner, cover her expenses, or maybe promise her love, harmony, family, and kids. But a woman should know his biology, his chemistry, and his psychology better than she knows the man! He has that sexual impulse that beats his intellect or conscience every time a sexual opportunity comes by. Again, that's not surprising, for we live in a sexually liberated environment where there are plenty of potential mates. Men's options for excitement and sexual pleasures are virtually endless. A woman cannot allow herself to fall in the man's traps or fall at his mercy. Remaining independent of the man is key to a woman's survival in the world and her personal success, since it's the only thing that can see her through tough times, for instance, when he'll no longer be there for her. From a biological and sociocultural standpoint of our times, woman's ideal companion, if she happens to have one, can never last forever. He will gradually exhaust himself and die like a candle in the wind along with his sexual fire.

But if family and kids are still something a woman desires, it does not necessarily mean her next step should be marriage. The marriage contract is extinguishing quietly because it's old-fashioned and cannot answer the need of the hour. The rules by which we play today have changed dramatically. Our lifestyles slackened, frenzied and diversified. Science and technology accelerate our pace and improve our standard of living. Limitations of time and place play minor roles or are not relevant at all. And there are plenty of opportunities to mingle and get to know new sexual partners. Our world has become fast, flat, and overly global. And in such a constellation, the traditional patriarchal family, as a solution, can no longer help. In the new circumstances that emerged, making a man commit to marriage would be like putting a butterfly in a cage, a useless thing. The marriage contract might also put the woman in the man's jail for a lengthy period, until eventually they'll blow up this cage, break it into pieces, and divorce. Only at this point it would be costly and much harder for the woman, for the man, and for everybody. Clearly, the best way to avoid this mess would be not to get on this foolish ride in the first place.

The marriage contract, based for the most part on interests, money, social and political manipulations, religious dictates, and old-fashioned norms should give way to brave relationships based on genuine friendship, mutual respect, and yes, also fulfilling sex. But even if, on the face of it, a core of sex, friendship, and mutual respect do exist between you, self-reliant woman, and your man, beware of men that are eager to sign a marriage contract or apply for a marriage license.

History shows that marriage has always been a perfect cover-up for underlying interests: be them political, economical, and also hereditary and biological. Don't be naïve. Ignoring the interests is like burying your head in the sand. You should be smart enough to ponder and connect the hidden dots of your relationship. Be true to yourself and never let the bells and whistles of the courtship and his chivalrous gestures spin your head.

If he's proposed, ask yourself first if perhaps he's interested to marry, because he wants you to work for him, he wants you to play the traditional women gender roles of taking care of the cleaning, ironing, cooking, and later raising the kids. Beware of anything that smacks traditional woman enslavement! During our postmodern times, both genders must fulfill the same roles. Ask yourself if perhaps he wants to marry because he wants you to answer his sex calls, even though his line might be busy with casual flirts. Or perhaps he's just unstable financially or immersed in debts. Perhaps he owes someone money? Perhaps he needs your money, or your father's financial support, or your mother's inheritance as a breath of fresh air because he's a loser? All these can be underlying causes to the man's decision to want a marriage despite his biology, physiology, and psychology, and sometimes even against his will or "love" per se. Such decisions show you that it’s not only men's natural biological inclination and behavior, or our postmodern times science and technology, or our abundant instantaneous social alternatives “to blame”—but there is much more into it.

2

The Cheater's Game

NESTERS & HUNTERS

I've just got off the phone from cheering up a newlywed colleague of mine, Amanda. She is thirty-six and recently married a twice divorced forty-year-old good looking lawyer. Now, she told me she caught her husband red-handed with a woman at a trendy bar in the Village. What a pain. It had not even been four months since their lavish wedding in Hawaii and he has been misbehaving right in front of her eyes. Not that the latest news surprised me. On the contrary, I took her prince charming for a sly dog from the moment I first met him at their wedding. But putting it aside for a moment: Amanda was literally devastated. Sobbing and sniffing, she channeled her rage into something that looked to me like a plot for revenge. What's more, she wanted me to call a number and find out who this "bitch" was, but I refused emphatically. "That's a waste of time." I told her. "You must understand ma cherie: You're not alone in this game, there's a male motive playing here like a worn out record. Most men cheat on their women whether they're married or not."

Want to know why? Strip a typical male naked and see what you get: a big lump of sexual instincts and hormones craving for satisfaction time and time again. That is the basic nature of a standard man. He's never fulfilled. He's constantly on the prowl for easy prey, ready for intercourse with him. And women should not pretend to be innocent here. Women, too, are ready to have sex with men especially in our postmodern and liberated epoch. But as a rule, unlike men, fewer women are likely to cheat on their men;[1] and specifically, fewer married women are likely to cheat on their husbands than the other way around.[2] Also unlike men, women usually don't look for the thrill of the chase in itself but would rather "dock" their guys and make them stay with them in a nest. Women usually prefer the stability of one man to going out to look for the next man.[3] Research shows that even those single women who play the sex game with men and change their partners as if they were socks usually have deeper intentions beyond sex.[4] Women are also known to develop an emotional connection or attachment to the sex partner after having sex with him[5] and are disturbed by "emotional infidelity" of the partner more than a "sexual infidelity."[6] So if there is an emotional attachment in men, it may show up during the courtship phase, before the sexual act. But after sex, most men are more interested in a good night sleep than in a talk with their sexual partner, and that might be the case until the next time they are interested in sex. This behavior of men leads to the conclusion that for men the hunting game is the most exciting part, followed by the sexual trophy. Any connection between male sex and emotions appears to be coincidental.

An interesting study conducted by neuroscientists from the Indiana University asked two groups of women: one group that had sexual partners and another group that did not, and likewise two groups of men, one group that had sexual partners and another group that did not—to evaluate photos of strangers of the opposite sex (women were asked to evaluate men, and men were asked to evaluate women) for traits such as realism, masculinity or femininity, attractiveness, or affect. The researchers found that women, who had sexual partners spent less time evaluating the photos of stranger men (which shows that these woman were less attentive to the men they saw in the pictures and were not interested in new men) than those women who did not have sexual partners—while the group of men who had sexual partners did not spend less time evaluating the photos of women, compared to the group of men that did not have sexual partners. This proves that these men were attentive to women and interested in them in any case. This research also suggests that women, on average, are relatively committed in their romantic relationships to their men, "which possibly suppresses their attention to and appraisal of alternative male partners".[7]

That's been just another example to the "sexual programming" of men. We can see again that while Mother Nature made males resemble hunters, she made women resemble nesters or collectors. Because women have the potential to give birth, naturally, they are gathering "resources and conditions" that will make their nest feel cozier and more conformable.[8] So, women would prefer a stable man who can assist them in their nesting efforts to a man who would jump from nest to nest. However, men's nature does not line up with such goals. Steadiness and stability are definitely not part of their modus operandi but brief sexual contacts preferably with physically attractive and youthful women certainly are.[9] So suppose they've built a nest with a woman, shortly after that, they might forget their vows, their promises, and their mutual plans and embark on an extra-curricular business, a fling, or a love affair. Show me a guy, even one believed to be an image of honesty who would refuse to a fling with a pretty "chick" who comes for a visit in his office scantily clad. Even if he's a well-respected senior citizen, renowned middle aged accountant, or a former priest, heaven forbid, and the woman is not, say, Angelina Jolie— he'll jump on the occasion as if he found a worthy treasure.

You can think of men as radios, if you want: always tuned in and continually transmitting and receiving sexual signals through their antennas. They feel it in the air everywhere, in the street, in the car, at work, after work. The game starts as soon as their signal is answered. Next, their antennas rise, along with their egos, to towers' heights. It can happen to them in the elevator when a sexy woman looks them over with her bedroom eyes, as much as when a female colleague compliments their new bowtie at work. It happens all the time, regardless of who they are, how old they are, where they live, what they do for a living, if they're rich and famous, married or not.

"I Did Not Have Sexual Relations with That Woman"

Of course, the richer and the more famous the guy is, the higher his chances are to actually catch new intercourse partners in his vicinity. Usually, that's a mixed blessing for such guys, though, because being in the public eye means all their sexual affairs are exposed from the inside out, and their dirty linens are quickly washed in public.

Remember what happened to former president Bill Clinton? One of his biggest embarrassments came in

1995 when Monica Lewinsky, then a twenty-two year old intern working in the White House, gave Mr. President, then a forty-nine year old middle-aged man, what his beastly instinct instructed him to want from her…; Although he claimed to be quite passive in this oral scene and insisted it was performed on him and not by him, which should not have been considered as "sexual relations" according to him[10] hard fact is that his legendary sentence "*I did not have sexual relations with that woman*" which later turned into a "masculine national anthem" and metaphor for the cheating of men—happened several times at various locations inside the White House.

With all due respect to former President Clinton, his innovation in the adultery business certainly broke new records. In the end, of course, he admitted that indeed he had some "inappropriate intimate relations" with that woman and was later impeached for a while by the House of Representatives and later acquitted by the Senate.[11] There has been a huge international buzz around his story, as the media glamorized the story even further. Being the talk of the town for quite some time, the story quickly turned into "the most coveted thing a man should do during his lifetime." And I would wager there had been no male in the entire universe that did not want to be so successfully treacherous as former President Clinton.

Before you plunge into any commitment with a guy, always remember that exactly like in the Clinton case, men are by nature doomed to look for sex in their vicinity and are always interested in sex in all its glorious forms. Thus what keeps men ticking during the courtship phase is the pure thrill of the chase, nothing more, nothing less. But once the chase is over and they get their kill, literally, it's game over for them. Men need to keep that thrill coming and going, and exactly for that reason, they're after variety, which is one of the most important features of our postmodern culture.

Research suggests that men spend more time than women in looking for short-term relationships, so as to minimally invest their resources and energy while maximizing their access to potential sexual mates.[12] Men feel reassured to know that they still have it with one woman as much as with the next. They expect women to take a number slip and stand in their lines. They feel that since they are men, it is their "prerogative" to have sex with whoever catches their fancy and exactly the way that they want it.

Men think that free sex, exactly like other resources and properties in society, is their own domain, unlike women who do not feel they are entitled to have sex as freely as men.

This feminine inhibition, among others, might result

from a social and cultural double standard that made women feel promiscuous and cheap whenever they wanted to have sex, either before marriage or during marriage. Whereas the same double standard made men feel reinforced by their decision to have sex and rewarded by society. The freedom to have sex was considered a purely male thing before modern times.[13] That is, from prehistoric times through the ancient times, the Middle Ages, the Renaissance, the age of the Enlightenment, and up through the sixties—women's sexuality has been a cultural taboo, concealed by society and condemned by it. And any decision to have sex, either premarital sex or through infidelity in marriage, coming from the side of the women, was, therefore, put in the closet for the greater part of human civilization.

But even today in the midst of the postmodern age and the highly industrial era, men feel more entitled than women to get free sex. While some men are "lucky" enough and are presented occasionally with plenty of sexual opportunities, other men are less blessed, but still on a constant prowl for adventures and surprises. But unexceptionally, all men discussed by the women who were interviewed for this project found it irresistible to say no to a "sexy young thing," a woman who showed even the slightest hint of interest in their masculinity. Most men treat such situations where the women might be interested in their "manly services" as a once-in-a-lifetime opportunity and joyfully go for the kill, until the next prey comes along.

This is what happened to South Carolina Governor Mark Sanford. In June 2009, this revered man went AWOL from his office without letting anyone know his whereabouts for six full days.[14] His family and close friends did not have a clue where the gentleman was and neither did his staff at the office. After massive media coverage of his bizarre disappearance, he suddenly reappeared and charmingly announced that he had been in Argentina with a woman with whom he was having an extramarital affair. He also admitted that while he was married he "crossed the lines in a handful of other opportunities".[15] A case that demonstrates, again, how the natural instincts of men to go from one kill to the next dictate their behaviors, notwithstanding any social conventions or expectations from their high ranking jobs or public careers.

Another sensational example is Tiger Woods, the US golf champion and one of the most successful golfers of all time. Look what happened to this role model. Like Sanford and Clinton, Woods, then thirty-four years of age, was famous, successful, and filthy rich. Like Clinton and Sanford, he was married to a beautiful woman. Why in the world should a guy like him embark on extramarital affairs with one woman after another? Because he's a man living in a world of sexual variety, craving of that sexual variety to boot. He did what he did, because it was so easy for him to do it. An iconic sports star, adored by millions, having long lists of female fans of every shape and form... all he had to do was just take his pick. But what helped him more was the fact that it was so easy for him to get away with it. Woods, who felt he was entitled to enjoy all the pleasures around him, after working so hard on his career, was simply hunting for variety, for new prey, for more spice and for more thrill, exactly like a typical male in nature.

Now don't get me wrong. I am not supporting Woods, Sanford, or Clinton's infidelity. I'm just giving you the bare facts. Men are doomed to cheat on women. Period. They are made for that. Period. Like some celebrities, sports stars, and high profile politicians, men tend to have sex outside their commitments or marriages, because they want excitement, and because they can, too. And exactly like these celebrities, most married men feel they will be able to survive and live well after their acts. But even though sex for variety is the prime reason for infidelity, most men cheat because they know for fact that their spouses will stand by their side no matter what after their infidelity act (like Hillary Clinton did,) and that's of course a big mistake. A woman should never accept a cheater by her side but instead get rid of him at the speed of light at the first sign of transgression.

Being weak and meek with a man while married in response to cheating can be emotionally devastating for the woman and can have negative physical implications as well.[16] But think of this: Why should a woman commit to a potential cheater in the first place through a marriage contract? Is it because she really wants to provide the perfect "happily married family" cover-up so her man can do whatever he likes most and can do best— sex with other women? Let's face it: The social institution of marriage is dying a much anticipated death. And we should let it die peacefully and never pray for its resurrection. The above examples demonstrate how marriage can bind women to cheating men and reduce them to nothing but alibis covering their famous spouses' fling after fling after fling.

DID I DO ANYTHING WRONG?

Studies show that the majority of men who cheat on their spouses do it purely for sexual reasons as compared to emotional reasons for women.[17] The tremendous increase in the number of women in the workplace, a direct result of women's liberation process, especially in the aftermath of the sexual revolution of the 1960s, and more openness in society toward sex, are important factors to understanding why cheating is easier to conduct. Even the not so rich and famous men today are occasionally presented with an amazing variety of potential sexual partners outside the home, both in their vicinity and online. And it doesn't matter if they are married or not, have amazing sex lives with their partners, are fathers to kids, or make $250K or more. Men are just after plurality. But interestingly, because the traditional values of patriarchal marriage are engraved so deeply in women's minds, some women who are cheated on by men, do not have a clue about their men's extra curricular affairs. On the contrary, these women tend to think that something in their relationship is not working, or even worse, they often blame themselves for not being good enough for their men. This is certainly a medieval line of thought. If your man is cheating on you, it would be stupid of you to blame yourself and not the man, on condition that you did not change your habits.

If a man were cheating on you, the worst thing to do would be to sound apologetic and ask yourself questions such as "did I do anything wrong?" Even if your sex life does not rock like it used to, and even if it doesn't create the same level of sparks, it does not mean he should have filled the gaps clandestinely with another woman. But the problem with men is they don't really accept that faithfulness should be a two way street, but rather believe that loyalty should be a woman thing, while sexual games should be their own. Again, this patriarchal mindset has been inherited by men from their fathers, grandfathers, and their great-grandfathers who used to live by patriarchal, androcentric, and essentially sanctimonious values and norms.

Remember, when cheating hits, feeling pity is like crying over spilt milk. It would never see you through the hard situation. So if he did what he did, make it clear to him unequivocally that there is no way back. Even if he says it has been one-time slip (this is usually their lame excuse, isn't it?) don't take it seriously. Like in the Sanford case, there have been probably more instances of the same kind, and it was just your first time to find out about it. But even if you take his word for it, there's nothing that can reassure you that it won't happen again.

Although cheating can be a really hard experience for a woman and her family, using a counseling service would probably not be the most helpful way to deal with it. This is because, usually, counselors tend to smooth things over between the woman and her man, and make her forgive and forget. Like a kindergarten teacher rebuking a naughty child, the traditional counselors I interviewed tended to advise against divorce and push for reconciliation, as the first stage. Perhaps the reason has to do with the fact that most counselors still represent the old-fashioned institution of marriage and therefore work in concert with the patriarchal family norms. The vast majority of the counselors urged the troubled woman to give her relationship boat that had clearly run aground a second shot. That is buying time for marriage and certainly not what most women want. If the woman turns to counseling to alleviate her own pain, that is, to share her emotions with the counselor, that's fine. But if she does it to reconcile her lousy relationship and make it last for more time, that's a different story. In any case, a woman should never accept infidelity in her home. There is no reason for a woman to subject herself to stress, emotional torture, and health risks, when she can instead invest her energy and time in finding a more compatible partner.

Send Him Away

Why carry on with a treacherous guy who exposes the woman to risks? For instance, what if the man sleeps with the woman without using a condom and later sleeps with his "official" partner or wife? As you probably know, the man's original mate might contract STDs, or worse. Many sexually contracted diseases continue to, despite the improvements of modern medicine, at best present unpleasant symptoms and life-long complications and, at worst, pose the risk of death. So there is really no reason for the woman to take this chance. Now what if the guy sleeps with his mistress and later she gets pregnant? And next, what if he uses his wife's bank account or their joint credit card to sponsor his mistress' lavish lifestyle? How should his wife handle that? If his wife makes a mistake and forgives and forgets, she will do nothing but reward the man's unfaithfulness, and it will surely happen to her again. But if, on the other hand, she leaves the stage right after the dirty act was played, she will be killing two birds with one stone. First she'll take her revenge and make him suffer, and second, she'll finally get rid of the man.

No old-fashioned patriarchal values of marriage, morality issues, phony ethics, and brainwashing from the media, the social institutions, and the states should make a woman stick to a man if he's cheated on her. After the man's cheating act, pursuing the former "perfect family" ideal would be like burying the head in the sand. Chances are the man will repeat his acts with the same woman or with another one, pretty soon.

So after he did what he did, it's time for the woman to strike a pose and teach him a lesson. She should say no to the traditional societal expectations from her as a woman to play her submissive gender role, usually "for the sake of her family," "for the sake of her kids," or for whatever the phony political-correct reason of the moment is. If the woman hated what the man did to her, there's no reason in the world why she should stick with him like nothing happened. She should be true to herself and assertive enough to hold her own and say "Enough is enough. We are through." The next step should be to dump him.

When you are unmarried, getting rid of a treacherous thing should be as easy as tossing an old shoe. Why repair it if it was both cheap and uncomfortable for you to wear? There are plenty of other classy shoes that can do the same job or even better. The variety is amazing today, and you can certainly find pair that will make you smile. This is another substantial benefit of never committing to a man through the contract of marriage. If he cheats on you, there's no legal alibi such as marriage to cover-up his acts like a veil. All you have to do is send him away without extra efforts and costly divorce attorneys. But if you are married, calling it off is a more intricate task, because you'll have to file for divorce, and that could be a mess. You'll need a lawyer who will carry a formal legal court action for you. You'll need to spend energy, time, and money on getting rid of him. But, thankfully today, most states have enacted the no-fault divorce statute which makes it easier for women to release from the marriage contract without having to prove to the court who was responsible for the marriage breakdown. Unlike before 1969, women today do not have to shed tears in front of the court to demonstrate they have been victimized by their husbands, even if they truly were.[18] They can just file unilaterally for divorce. However, unfortunately, in some states, a separation or a "cooling period" of living apart from the husband for some time before granting a divorce is still required.

Despite the fact that under the "no fault" divorce statute today a woman does not need to prove in court that her husband has been cheating on her or abusing her sexually, emotionally, or otherwise committing unsavory acts in order to divorce—the court of law still looks closely at the responsibility of the spouses for breaking down marriage when it comes down to splitting the martial property and joint money equitably between the spouses. This is because the marriage contract is hinged on the joint ownership presumption. In some states, the court still needs to see that the relationship is no longer viable and that irreconcilable differences caused irremediable breakdown.[19] The patriarchal institution of marriage, it seems, is still interested that women will stick with their men and that the marriage contract will remain effective, rather than letting the women get out of the bond and setting them free. We will later explore why the institution of marriage regulated by the states wants women to remain bound to their men even when marriage seems to be crippled. For now, let's keep in mind that the issue of responsibility for the breakdown of marriage is still considered in some states and seriously weighted when marital rights such as alimony and child support for the custodian parent are to be allocated to the woman and potentially to the kids of the couple.

There's no reason in the world why a self-sufficient, independent, and successful young woman today should set her relationship in stone through a marriage contract. Not only are legal commitments useless when it comes to obligations of men, they might also be big headaches when the women attempt to break free. Had there not been a marriage contract, things would be a lot easier for women like my colleague, Amanda. She could absolutely spare much energy, time, and money invested in the bureaucratic process of divorce. And, thinking of it, she and her husband did not have kids or marital accumulated properties together to split, just their separate properties. Had there been mutual kids or marital properties, things would be worse for her and women like her. And this is especially critical when powerful women are concerned—women who have separate properties, careers, and an independent path in life. (In our postmodern age, being financially self-sufficient is definitely a must for a woman. When a woman is financially self-made, she does not need to depend on her man's marital benefits, financial support, or alternatively, institutional benefits, or government aid.) Currently, when a self-made woman within marriage files for divorce, she must hope that the court of law will be fair enough to spare dividing her separate property or money, that is property or money she had before marriage. But if the court of law is less fair, such a woman might find herself at a disadvantage. To avoid that, the rule of thumb would be to spare marriage. No matter how old the woman is, what she does for a living, and what her annual income is, the best way would be to prevent problems rather than cure them later upon a painful divorce.

THE TECHNOLOGY OF CHEATING

Men's cheating is as old as mankind. However, in past centuries it used to require a lot of courage, maneuvers, and also resources to carry out an illicit affair and avoid detection. As far as men were concerned, the institution of marriage permitted infidelity. However, for the women, the gender roles were stricter and sexist, in the sense that women who cheated on their men were treated as "whores" in society, for instance in the Victorian age.[20] From time immemorial cheating has been a men's thing. But unlike today, in the past, the technological means used to be limited and did not work so much in favor of infidelity.

Take for instance transportation and communication. During the Medieval Age, people used to travel by horses, and only in the late fourteenth century with the improvement of roads, the more affluent could afford traveling by carriage. At that time, most of the mingling and the weaving of romantic ties were regional, physical, and face to face. Delivery through an intermediary was also an option, and wherever faraway cheaters were concerned, the post office was also to their aid. Long before the industrial revolution, cheaters used to send letters overseas by postal services that used very slow land and water transport. Before the modern trains, ships, and aviation services were in place—cheaters living at a distance from one another had to wait weeks and sometimes months for their love message to arrive at the destination; and with their anticipation, their passion often died.

The advent of the phone in 1880 undoubtedly revolutionized the speed factor in the cheating business, making love talks instantaneous on both ends, but still, costly to an average pocket. Following the industrial revolution in the later part of the eighteenth century, with enormous mechanization, improvement in railways and road systems, improvement in the steam engine, invention of the internal combustion engine, electricity, and invention of the airplane in 1903, along with lower costs incurred on each of those technologies—cheating, as a social phenomenon, gathered tremendous momentum. If before the industrial revolution cheating had been rather cumbersome, slow, and almost unbearable—in the modern era, after the revolution, with tremendous improvement in technological means, cheating gradually became simple to plot, elegant to carry out, and easy to maintain.

Greater improvements in technology during the twentieth century have steadily paved the way for swifter, cheaper, and much more sophisticated cheating—until it become a sweeping phenomenon at the end of the twentieth century and the start of the twenty-first. The advent of the jumbo jet in 1970—carrying over four hundred people at once and the deregulation of airline lines which made flying an ordinary expense—have further accelerated the mobility of cheaters. Cheaters could fly to their mistresses much faster and also cheaper without feeling remorse of any kind.

Satellites and fiber optics further reduced the cost of long distance communication to a fraction of former rates, allowing cheaper infrastructure for communication. Cellular phones and other radio devices connected cheaters momentarily to one another. But the most incredible technological breakthrough was definitely in the field of microelectronics, with the invention of the transistor which allowed for packaging electrical appliances into tiny packages, and with the microchip that was invented in the late 1960s. These inventions allowed for the production of pocket size cellular devices that later became wireless, portable, and accessible to all, anytime and from any point in space.[21] These devices were, and still are, the cheaters' trump cards.

In the midst of the 1980's, when the PC arrived on the scene and was reduced in cost in the 1990s, cheating reached new heights. And so in the late twentieth century and at the beginning of the twenty-first, with the aid of higher computer capacity, huge storage volumes for devices, fast communication protocols, wireless technologies, and miniscule computerized systems—every cheater on earth could have the most cutting edge technologies and use them to his best advantage. With greater industrialization and innovation in communication, transportation, telecommunication and aviation—which boosted the commerce, the trade, the investment, the overall standard of living, medicine, human longevity, entertainment, and leisure on a global scale— there also came an incredible amount of cheating.

Among other influences, cheating was a byproduct of industrialization, tech innovation, and modernization of the US and the western world. It could be carried out much more efficiently than in the past, much faster, much cheaper, and almost without limitations of time and place. The global technological world of our times has definitely boosted the phenomena of cheating, allowing for greater independence and freedom for partners, greater interactions between the sexes, as well as considerable variety of potential sexual partners.[22]

Today, at the start of the twenty-first century, it has become extremely comfortable for men to maintain their extracurricular affairs. With faster communications technologies, wireless systems, GPS, Internet cell phones, instant email services, online communities, and social networking websites such as Facebook and Twitter that are all the rage—the process of interacting, meeting, and intermingling culminated into a full-fledged cheating business, both virtual and real—a true relationship outside a relationship (or inside a relationship depending on what side of the aisle you're standing). With long distances now covered in fractions of a few hours, married men have the advantage of making trans-country and trans-Atlantic "business trips" and returning the same day or the day after, leaving their kids with their faithful mothers at home. When these men get home, some complain about "terrible jetlags and headaches" because of the hard business trips they have been on. Which might be true—only it was a different kind of hard business they were into.

With reduction in costs, not only could the high-society cheaters afford such business trips, but so could the ordinary middle class women and men. And as soon as the modern technology was fully adopted by the masses, it has become commonplace for cheating men to have lovers or mistresses on the side, parallel to their existing official commitments. Great distances are now compensated through fast, convenient, and relatively cheap flights from place to place, reinforced by speedy emails, messenger talks, and free web phone conversations, supported by webcams from whatever location men are in, be it their office, a coffee shop in the street, a hotel room in Casablanca, or their bedroom at home.

Never in the past has cheating been such a popular

fad as it is now. A simple text message allows men to take their lovers virtually everywhere with them. Portable computers, laptops, and wireless connectivity have made men far better equipped to carry out multiple relationships in parallel. Various dating portals, sex, and porn websites, have also added to the woes of innumerable women who just can't keep up with the pace of what's going on with their men. A few women I recently talked to have told me how their partners spent more and more time in front of the computers after they get back from work. In fact, I've heard of an amazing number of friendships and marriages crashing down into pieces because the guys inevitably started having virtual affairs with women they met on the social networking websites. Of course, most of these virtual affairs quickly turned into real life romances the moment these cheaters stepped into the real world. As it turns out, cheaters did not spare their best efforts in translating the virtual episodes into real ones. It appears that cheaters knew how to use the latest technology of cheating to their best advantage and operate online and offline simultaneously, through fixing creative secret getaways, attending night romps, arranging rendezvous, and, as happy as lark, returning to their nests at home like paragons of virtue.

TECHNOLOGY IS FIGHTING BACK

Unfortunately, some male cheaters still underestimate women's power today. My interviews reveal that some cheaters still foolishly assume that because they've been using sophisticated high technology, they can't go detected in the real world. That's undoubtedly a chauvinistic line of thought. It is crystal clear today that if technology can facilitate the cheating process, it can likewise help in tracking down the cheaters deeds. But some cheating men prefer the macho explanation instead, degrading women through assuming they are not smart enough or fit enough to use "their technology" to track them down.

Like other properties in society, men see technology as a men's dominion rather than a universal asset. That, again, is a patriarchal mindset rooted in the belief that women are less intelligent than men. Such a sexist idea was particularly popular with the advent of Darwinism and Freudism in the modern society at the middle of the nineteenth century and the beginning of the twentieth one.

Both Darwin's evolution by natural selection theory and Freud's psycho-sexual theory saw the women's intellectual and psycho-sexual development as inferior to men's. So the next time you have the slightest suspicion that your guy is cheating on you, definitely make this sexist assumption of men your reference point: You shall be harnessing the same "man's" advanced technologies for setting your cheater a trap. Your cheater must forget all these stereotypes and prejudices about women being less competent or less intelligent than men. Generally speaking, getting rid of the sexist "weaker sex" stereotype altogether can be in favor of every woman and particularly the one who has been cheated on.

In the midst of this hi-tech revolution, a woman should definitely keep up with the pace and take advantage of the latest technologies and tech innovations available. In this retaliation game, the woman should fight using her brains. If she suspects her guy is cheating on her, she can harness technology to spy on him. A tactic that proves to be working is secretly checking on the guy's "Short Message Service" (SMS) on his mobile devices. The latest in SMS is called "sexting," sending sexually laced texts and photos. So a woman might be interested to look for evidence of virtual sexts on his mobile phone, for instance, when he goes to the bathroom or even takes a paper or a book to the restroom. Being decisive and acting fast is key here, otherwise the guy might figure out he is being tapped. If the guy is too hooked to his mobile device even at the restroom, or takes it with him to shave in the bathroom, that would be another red light for the woman.

If a woman suspects her man is cheating, she should not give up on her search, even if intentionally he's made it extremely difficult for her to detect what he did; she should be agile and find alternative methods. For instance, mobile service providers have call records which can be accessed upon a special request. A woman can contact the man's mobile provider and ask to send his call records directly to her mailbox or by snail mail. Then, after the records arrive, she'll have to sift through these numbers using call duration and time of call as parameters of reference. A more sophisticated method would be to use existing online open-source software to secretly tap the guy's phone and monitor his calls, texts, and even emails. Here, the best way would be to pre-install the tracking program on a new cell phone or mobile device and gift it to the guy with a broad smile. The guy would probably be delighted with his new toy and won't be afraid to show it off to his friends. Only the next time he does what he does with the woman, the tech savvy woman will have more than a clue with whom he'd been hanging around and what he'd been up to. If still ineffective, the woman can certainly hire a private investigator as the last resort. That would be a little costly, but well worth the price and effort, especially if the man is framed in the end. But, before that, the woman must be absolutely positive to have had used all the available technological means and her common sense to find out all the truth.

Clearly, no woman should end up like former South Carolina governor's wife, Mrs. Sanford, who found out about her husband's affair with the Argentinean lover only after several years[23], or like Maria Shriver, former wife of Arnold Schwarzenegger, who had found out about her husband's affair with the housekeeper and about their mutual boy, only after 20 years during which the woman had been working in their house![24] Every woman should be familiar with the "technology of cheating" and use it to find out things about her man.

No question, that's a lousy situation for the woman to be in, in the first place, to suspect the man she's been loyal to is cheating. But life is no picnic and is not fair to everyone at all times. And sometimes it's better for the woman to get off the train before it takes the wrong direction. So when the man is caught hitting on another woman, the best solution would be to cut it off with him. Putting up with a lousy relationship where the woman suspects the guy she trusted the most in cheating is not a healthy situation for the woman to be in. If the woman is committed to the legal contract of marriage, she must know for sure before filing for divorce whether he'd been cheating on her or not.

However, if the woman is single, that would be a lot easier for her to cope with the situation by splitting momentarily. Nonetheless, every woman, no matter single or not, should definitely strive to draw a clear-cut conclusion, only black and white and no grey tones. Did he or did he not cheat on her? He did not? Good for him. She can kiss him goodnight and turn off the light. He did? Heaven, there is no other choice for her but to tell him good riddance.

Apparently, cheating has been, and still is, a sweeping sociocultural phenomenon in the western civilization. Closely associated with it is—first, men's natural predisposition to look for sexual variety whenever and wherever they can, notwithstanding age, ethnicity, religion, occupation, former commitment to a partner, or income. Naturally speaking, every man is a potential cheater. While the rich and famous appear to use their financial and social prestige arsenal to get laid with more women and also more frequently—every man is on a constant prowl for new sexual mates and new exciting games.

The second factor is the media that provides comprehensive coverage of cheating celebrities and role models, such as Tiger Woods and Arnold Schwarzenegger—as cultural heroes after their cheating deeds. The media does it vicariously by bringing to viewers juicy stories about these stars, stories that serve to promote the networks' ratings and profits, on the one hand, and to boost the celebrities' popularity, sexiness, and success on the other.

Why was Tiger Woods voted "the athlete of the decade" by the Associated Press Sports Writers after admitting to a host of affairs with various women and after deciding to take a break from golf?[25] Why did the media give him such a magnificent honor?

Apparently, the media and the culture are still appreciative of infidelity that is considered "manly" and “brave” when it comes from the side of the man, not the side of the woman. That reflects a patriarchal attitude in our society and culture, which is clearly playing against women today, as it has played for centuries.

Third, the communication technology, computation, transportation, and aviation had a tremendous effect on cheating, especially after the industrial revolution in the middle of the eighteenth century. With the aid of technology, cheating has become affordable, easier to plot, and much more elegant to maintain, both in the physical and the virtual spaces. But, in spite of the fact that cheating has been elevated to the ranks of an "institution" today, some women still commit to their guys in traditional marriage, a thing that they later considerably regret.

3

An Illusion Called Wedding

PATRIARCHAL WINDS

On Saturday afternoon I went with my friend Jenny to a picnic in the Central Park. I brought a red Spanish wine and Jenny prepared a plate of assorted cheeses, fresh veggies, and rye bread. We placed a blanket on the grass and let our celebration begin. We raised a few toasts, first to health and wealth, second to success, and the last one to freedom. Oh, yes, and then a little tiny extra one to happiness as well... Before long, we both felt a little more cheerful and relaxed.

Then Jenny told me a secret about her older sister, Donna. "Donna is about to divorce Sean after twenty years of marriage!"

"Oh Really?" I tried to sound surprised. The news was not hard to believe. Donna's husband was both a womanizer and a workaholic. And it always amazed me how they managed to stay together. I've never said so, but their relationship looked quite strange to me, like an amateur theater show with the characters either too artificially perfect or too perfectly artificial.

Donna was a full-time mother and a part-time journalist. Her husband, Sean, was a full-of-himself gynecologist. He was actually very successful and loved his job, and probably his women clientele so much that he never missed an opportunity to stay late at the office to deal with "emergencies" that always came up. In fact, Jenny said that he used to spend long days, and occasionally nights, away from home. And as far as their twin boys were concerned, Sean never invested too much time or energy in helping them grow up, so Donna had to do it on her own. But now, with the boys grown, spreading their wings and off at college, and after she hadn't seen him in bed the other night, she finally made a decision. She wanted out. Self-assured in her ability to start over, she finally accepted a standing job offer to join her editorial team in Manhattan for a full-time position.

Coupled with Donna's decision to take her own independent path in life came a strong disbelief in the institution of marriage. Donna felt like she had been misled to believe that marriage was the right thing for herself and for her family. She felt she had been tricked into accepting that standing by her husband, including when the relationship faltered and failed, was not only the right thing—it was the best thing.

The institution of marriage, the government, the states, the law, the religion, the culture, the media—all these "syringes of society" had injected these ideas so deeply into her mind that she couldn't help but follow their dictates: Marry a guy (or, even better, marry up) give birth to a few kids, do your best to be a good wife, a great mother, and a perfect homemaker, serve your man sexually in bed, and stick by him through thick and thin. But you had better keep quiet whenever your man screws up, because your family is "sacred". And the rule of thumb is unity, security and stability—meaning your family must stay intact no matter what. You are taught to sacrifice and compromise to protect your family. You are taught to subordinate your personal interests and goals in life to the institution of marriage in order to serve the "greater good." In other words, you are taught to give up on your personal choices, to forget about your ambitions, compromise your rights, choke your feelings, and suffer.

This awkward "ideal family" concept has been fed to women for generation after generation as the ultimate blessing. Women are manipulated to think that the institution of marriage is the cornerstone of modern civilization, that the perfect family will teach them right from wrong, and that the family will see them through tough times.

Occasionally, women are also presented with additional reassuring concepts. Marriage is immaculate, innocent, and harmonious, they say. Marriage is the greatest culmination of “love”. But, guess what? It's a lie. The institution of marriage is nothing but a social delusion. It is a humankind invention. So perfectly concocted and served to us, marriage is believed to be the "real thing" whereas, in fact, it has been all made up.

The truth about marriage is that it is a total make-believe most people learn to live with without questioning why. But not only isn't patriarchal marriage the ultimate blessing for women, their families, their communities, their cities, their states, their country, or the entire universe—it's actually the most inappropriate solution today.

The patriarchal marriage is asynchronous with our time. It is outdated and outmoded. Old-fashioned marital values and morals cannot hold in an ever changing shaky world. Skyrocketing divorce rates are a perfect demonstration of this point. All the more, the patriarchal marriage is highly against men's natural inclinations to have multiple sexual partners and be continually on the hunt, notwithstanding marital status. On top of that, Marriage smacks from politics and is maneuvered by men in position of power in social, cultural, and especially economic spheres. Consequentially, marriage turned into a sexist and a highly manipulative institution. Since the middle of the twentieth century the patriarchal marriage has turned unstable. Now, at the outset of the twenty-first century, marriage is crumbling apart. It is eroding brick by brick, like a deck of cards. It appears that marriage has lost its credibility in society today, among other reasons, due to its underlying politics, interests, and manipulations.

The patriarchal ideas behind the institution of marriage can be rather harmful. They date back to biblical times, when women were possessions, owned by men like properties. Back then, women had no natural rights but to "be fruitful and multiply" and, of course, take care of the kids.[1] Later, in the ancient and classical times, the patriarchal institution governed by authoritative men developed this idea further. They saw the submission of the wives and the kids to the husbands as a microcosm of the submission of the entire family to the state. The Greek and Roman empires favored men's pubic lives and their devotion to the state to men's obsession with sexual pleasures, promiscuity, and prostitution, all of which were prevalent.[2]

Unlike today, where the institutions and the states have the ability to take care of nearly every citizen—in ancient times, it was essentially the role of the family. The patriarchal regulation of sexual, reproductive, and familial matters was preferred to losing control of the citizens. Indeed, the concept of family could play an important part in the order of the state, hadn't the patriarchal family been proposed as a remedy. In 330 BCE, the ancient Greek philosopher Aristotle wrote in his book *Politics*[3] that the perfect family should be a model for the organization of the state. He preached that humans should progress naturally from the family, through small villages, to the Polis or the ultimate order of the city-state—a model that was meant to cure the malignancies of his generation. But he also mentioned that the courage of a man should be evaluated by his ability to command a woman and get her to obey.

It's hard to believe, but even today at the start of twenty-first century, the concept of patriarchal family as obedient to the state, and the mother and kids as obedient to the father, are still taken seriously. Several patriarchal straight jacketed rules linger on as well. The patriarchal institution of marriage regulated by the states still regards the "pater," or the father, as the main authoritarian leader around which the nucleus of the family should be arranged with regard to legal rights, social status, and finances. For instance, stay-at-home mothers in the U.S. still get their health insurance coverage through their husbands' employers, and some rights and benefits (tax benefits, family benefits, immigration benefits, and more) depend on being tied to a man through a marriage contract.

Apparently, the modern institution of marriage is interested that women will tie themselves contractually to men and denies unmarried couples from gaining equal "marital" rights and benefits. This old-fashioned institution still expects women to subdue themselves to men and to the state through the marriage contract.

Despite the long strides taken in women's liberation and women's equal participation in the workforce parallel to their careers as mothers—some men still regard women as secondary, an idea first articulated by the feminist philosopher and founder of contemporary feminism Simone de Beauvoir (1908-1986) back in 1949. In her book "*The Second Sex,*"[4] de Beauvoir criticized the "destiny traditionally offered to women by society" through socialization into the feminine gender roles which made women focus on their looks rather than on education, career, or fulfillment of personal goals.

However, despite the best efforts by prominent feminist revolutionaries who paved the way for women's emancipation, among them Mary Wollstonecraft (who advocated for women's education in the eighteenth century), Lucy Stone, Susan B. Anthony, and Elisabeth Cady Stanton (who advocated for women's right to vote in the nineteenth century), Margaret Sanger (who started the birth control revolution with the pill in the twentieth century), as well as the aforementioned Simone de Beauvoir and many other women's rights advocates—women are still expected today to compromise on their careers, self-aspirations, and also privacy. For instance, some women are expected to retain the last names of their husbands rather than keep their own names after the wedding. And once their kids are born, more often than not, the kids are given their father's surnames not their mother's. Although the naming issue might seem minor at first glance, and although a growing number of women today hyphenate their names—it is definitely symbolic. It symbolizes the patriarchal heritage and the coercive nature of the institution of marriage. Many remnants of this kind are still with us today, despite being inconsistent with our postmodern generation.

Fact is that parts of society are patriarchal in worldview today and still expect women to grab onto traditional gender roles that look more "becoming" on women, such as being the only caretakers for the family and the kids. This expectation persists despite the emancipation of women, despite the sexual revolution, and despite the achievement of equal rights in a variety of spheres (i.e., politics, education, and business.) A successful businesswoman and forty-three year old mother I recently spoke to told me how she was summoned by her daughter's principal, because, apparently, her daughter went to school with her long curly hair untied and uncombed for three consecutive days:

"I was away on a business trip and Dave [her partner and a stay-at-home dad] was taking care of Lily. But it was I who got the phone call from school and was practically blamed for my daughter's untidiness! It was like: "can't you take care of your kid, woman?'"

Obviously, remnants of patriarchal straight jacket rules are rather persistent, even today, despite the great advancement in science, technology, and women's liberation. This is the case because some elements of society, namely, the government, the states, and the religious institutions, along with legal and cultural weapons that include the media (radio, television, the printed press, and the web), in addition to some businesses and establishments, such as the scientific (research labs), academic (institutes, colleges, and universities), and even the aesthetic (museums and galleries) establishments—are still very much interested in men's grasp and men's control of the most prestigious and also profitable power channels of society.

The patriarchal heterosexual nuclear family is, thus, preferred to the emerging alternative family structures—families of the postmodern nature where the individual is key to the familial structure, not the government, the states, or the corporations. Such families include the single parent family, the same-sex family, the families that adopt kids, and the families that "live apart together" (LAT, where each of partners maintains a separate household) which are all scrutinized with a suspicious eye by the existing patriarchal order for their "unreliable," "unstable," and essentially, "experimental" nature.

But how does the patriarchal infusion of thoughts work? The patriarchal means to achieve the desired social order goes through a sweeping cultural propaganda. Through filtering down ideas about the "perfect family" and communicating them to the public—the institution of marriage attracts more and more believers to its ranks.

From kindergarten kids playing traditional gender roles with planes (for boys) and kitchen-sets (for girls), through family car ads propagating perfect conjugal harmony, to Mills and Boon romantic novels—people are deluded to believe that these filtered messages about the "ideal family" are true. Not only are they true, the patriarchal make-belief goes, but they are also good, moral, and beautiful—just because they represent the interests of the "entire society." But, guess what? Again, it's a misconception. The patriarchal interests do not represent at least half of the population, which consists of women. Therefore, such overly tendentious ideas are never communicated impartially, in a way that both women and men would be able to see the underlying motives, the masked interests, and the politics. These ideas are communicated vicariously, through various popular means, such as through television, radio, art, movies, plays, and advertising, as much as through the scientific and the academic establishments—which are all fueled by the ultimate artillery: money. "Men's money," and lots of it.

And so with sleight of hand, the patriarchal society succeeds in its beyond the surface motives and interests that keep our society a "society of men" for the benefit of men. The truth about what marriage is and what marriage is for is, thus, deliberately concealed. The fact that most of the childrearing burden still falls on women, not on men, is never mentioned. The fact that women need to invest much more time and energy in raising kids, which equates to further lost income for women, is also silenced. And the fact that women are still expected to sacrifice their self-development and self-fulfillment for the "sake of the family" is put to rest.

Despite the achieved emancipation, the institution of marriage, by means of the marriage contract, still expects women to subdue themselves to men and their kids above all: above work, above study, above hobbies, above their dreams.

To keep the marriage boat afloat, women often compromise far more than men do. Despite the alleged equality in the workplace, wage gaps still exist with women earning seventy-eight cents on every dollar a man earns for the same qualifications and job in the year 2010.[5] This is an unacceptable fact. And it is closely related to marriage, because working mothers are still discriminated against working fathers for the same qualifications and jobs.[6] However the patriarchal institution of marriage prefers the more "distilled" picture of the nuclear family being an embodiment of the American dream and of marriage as the most beautiful and harmonious solution for relationships based on "love".

But the truth of the matter is that never before in history has the institution of marriage been naive. It has always been immersed in interests—social, political, and economic ones.

WHEN WEDDING MEETS INTEREST

Looking back at history, we can see that the institution of marriage and naivety never went hand in hand. The traditional patriarchal family has been manipulated by social, political, and economic interests. The patriarchal family of ancient times was deeply rooted in the ancient religious traditions (Judeo-Christian, Roman Catholic, and Protestant).[7] This type of family had clear interest in procreation as a means to religious and cultural propagation and preservation. Maintaining social-political power was critical, and the patriarchal family was the most basic unit to accomplish that.

It appears that in the past, the traditional marriage functioned as a social-political establishment. This fact did not change across time. Like the ancient family, the pre-industrial family, too, assigned childcare, and later, education of the kids to the women, while physical protection and providing for the family roles were assigned to men. Beyond these traditional roles, during most of history, the family unit had to cope with all the roles that today are assigned to the government and social institutions, such as social security, healthcare, and welfare for family members, as well as care of the elderly and sick. The traditional pre-industrial family had clear interests in landholding, producing food, controlling labor, maintaining the social status of the family, and regulating the inheritance to the next generations in the most productive way.[8]

During the seventeenth and the eighteenth century, families were expected to be arranged in monogamous nuclear units. Apparently, the Enlightenment movement that sought rationality, logic, and general order behind every act in social life had a powerful effect on society.[9] This quest for order and reason in all aspects of society sat quite comfortably with the ideals behind the patriarchal family, which was, in essence, hierarchal and orderly. The marriage flourished back then, due to its alleged rationality, logic, and the general order that were assumed to come with the marital commitment. The patriarchal marriage was believed to impose fewer burdens and fewer threats on society from political, sociocultural, and economical standpoints. Social order, abidance to the law, respect and obedience to the patriarch in response to all the decisions he made for the family were key concepts. The patriarchal institution was thus highly interested in the "balancing power" of marriage as weighting against the rising power of the modern science and the wonders of technology with their inherent freedom and threat.

In the aftermath of the Industrial Revolution, in the later part of the eighteenth century, patriarchal interests continued to lead the way through stricter allocation of men's and women's roles. While men of the household ventured out to work outside home, women stayed at home to maintain the household and take care of the kids.

Within the Victorian family, the role of the father was to provide money for the family (never subjecting his wife to breadwinning) through spending long hours at work, to mediate between the public and domestic domains, to keep informed about the world and bring this information home, and set the moral standards[10] while the role of the mother was to raise the kids, educate them according to patriarchal moral standards, take care of the household, and provide sex to her man.

While the industrial family enjoyed improved machinery, transportation, communication means, and general improvement in the standard of living—the authority of the patriarchal family still remained in place. It was the father who provided for his family and the mother who stayed at home. Due to the rat race, the father spent much less time with the kids and was remote to them, and the mother continued to compensate for that through never ending homemaking and caretaking chores. While in the post-industrial and modern family the responsibilities for healthcare, welfare, and education of the kids gradually passed from the family to states, public institutions, and private corporations—the division of roles continued to be gendered and the authority of the father continued to lead the way.

And while the Industrial Revolution did open a bridge toward individuality within relationships, due to fewer duties that the family unit had to take care of, the patriarchal family continued to be an important pillar in Western society. Undoubtedly, the new industrial era allowed more freedom and invited both women and men to escape from the marriage cell (for instance, through cheating on the spouse), but for the most part, such breaches were viewed as violations of the standard marital law, the accepted morals and ethics, and therefore, denounced by the modern society.

Throughout history, marriage has been a tool in the hands of patriarchal institutions to attain their social and political order. The oppression of women has been used as a means to impose their authority. For the most part, patriarchal institutions restricted women's natural rights and social opportunities. They denied women from having rights and any political or economic power.

From a legal standpoint, throughout most of the nineteenth century, the legal coverture was in place in the United States and Britain.[11] These laws denied women their legal rights upon marriage, merging the wives' rights with their husbands' rights. For instance, married women could not serve as breadwinners, own their own properties, make contracts or wills, and alternatively, exit marriage if they wanted. Back then, women, like properties, were in men's hands. Furthermore, the law did not offer them any protection from physical or emotional abuse in marriage, and rape within marriage was exempted from criminal prosecution.[12]

Gender roles within marriage continued to be imposed on women in the twentieth century as well, for instance through the Head and Master laws in the

US which denied women from making any decisions about the assets and the properties they owned jointly with their husbands.[13] Shamefully, the patriarchal interests and the oppressive tactics used against women to attain such interests lingered until the later part of the twentieth century. Only toward the end of the century the legal marital responsibilities were freed from traditional gender roles and the rape exemption in marriage was removed.[14]

During the twentieth century, despite the gradual improvement in women's legal status, women's movements' efforts, women's suffrage, participation in education, and the growing involvement at work—Western society continued to infuse the same patriarchal ideals about marriage, especially after the Second World War. After the war, the patriarchal institutions embarked on sweeping campaigns aimed at convincing those women who started working during the war to return to the home front.[15]

This home front propaganda, among others, was meant to take back the jobs possessed by women during the war. Another goal of the propaganda was to show to the world, and especially to the Soviets, how victorious, prosperous, and happy American life was after the war, in comparison to the communistic poverty and wretchedness. At this point, building up families where the men were working nine to five in the emerging factories and multinational corporations and the women were staying home, raising the kids, and waiting for the men to come back in their motor cars—became the most coveted dream. Here again, the heterosexual, patriarchal, and nuclear family was perceived as the ultimate symbol of security and stability, prosperity, and success at a national level. Of course, such ideals burst at their seams, later on, with the baby boom era. But until then, the monogamous, nuclear, patriarchal order continued to set the social tone.

For the most part of human history, marriage has been a matter of interest. The patriarchal institutions used marriage as a tool to accomplish their social, political, and economic goals. In most cases, the traditional patriarchal marriage bonds were effective means to preserve the family wealth and achieve social prestige, attain political power and social order and even secure tribal or national alliances.[16] The most salient aspects of patriarchal marriage were political and economic, especially for the wealthy who concocted marriages with foreign provinces or foreign nations to increase their social connections and boost their political influence. The patriarchal marriages were also effective tactics of protecting the holdings of the family and conquering land and possessions without needing a war.

Purely political marriages also happened, and women, too, took active part in their plot, especially in light of their inferior position against men in the patriarchal hierarchy. Indeed, some women married wealthier men in order to gain stable conditions and reliable breadwinners for the homes, to protect the family and the kids, as was expected. Like men, women were interested in gaining good in-laws and promoting their social prestige.

But the upper hand was never the women's or the men's alone, but that of the governments, the states, and the nations, and their social, political, and economic institutions that used all the available strategies and tactics to harness traditional marriage to their political ends. They used the available weapons, such as media, law, and the business world to attain full control of women, their sexual choices, their reproduction, their family, their health and wealth, their education, their career, their habits, their hobbies, their leisure, their entertainment, and their thoughts and actions as well. It seems that for their imperialistic ends, the means were always justified. And so they stood imperiously behind this misleading illusion, making women think it was for their own good.

THE PATRIARCHAL COMPLEX

Never in the history of humankind has the patriarchal marriage been natural to people, on the contrary. Exactly like "love," marriage is just another purely social phenomenon created by humans and spread by them; communicated, coordinated, and regulated. Being artificial and infective, patriarchal marriage possessed destructive power, not only in its ability to repress women physically, emotionally, professionally, economically, and legally—but also in its ability to spoil successful partnerships. Patriarchal marriage has both the ability to depress good choices couples make about one another and the ability to impose destructive decisions on couples.

Take a look at the following example. Veronica, one of the women I recently interviewed for the book, shared with me her relationship story. She told me she had an excellent physical, emotional, and intellectual relationship with her boyfriend, Steve, whom she was dating seriously for over two years before they decided to tie the knot officially. But when the idea of marriage came up, Veronica faced rejection from Steve's family. His family believed that because she did not belong to the same socioeconomic "ivy league" they thought they belonged to—marrying her was not even an option for him. Just to clarify: Veronica is an attractive young woman, a Harvard business school graduate who works as an economist for one of the leading investment firms. But, yes, her father was a tailor in Philly, and her mother still lives somewhere in Romania with her three younger brothers, two sisters, ten sheep and five cows. Perhaps her rural background was what frightened them the most, or the fact she was not purely Christian. For one reason or another, Veronica was denied from entering marriage with him, even before they formally applied for a marriage license.

Veronica's case is nothing special. Every day, thousands of couples are kept from marrying their partners by their close communities due to different kinds of sociocultural and political concerns that have to do with extended family issues, health issues, class issues, religious matters, racial concerns, cultural incongruities, their reputation in the community, and so forth. On the other hand, very unfit couples are occasionally encouraged to marry or even forced into marriage to later find themselves trapped. Such unfit connections are usually welcomed by the extended families, local communities, and the phony institution of marriage as a whole, for their ability to answer their "public interests" rather than serve individuals' interests. Evidently, marriage has immanent destructive power to impose unnatural decisions on both women and men, decisions driven by concessions to social interests.

Not only can the patriarchal marriage repress the most natural choices couples make and reduce them to social or political players—it can also foster the development of primordial complexes within the family as per the Freudian psycho-sexual theory. While Sigmund Freud is definitely not our role mode here, if we make his Oedipal Complex theory our reference point, for this matter, perhaps a lesson can still be learned. According to the Oedipal theory, boys, and young kids in general, might want to kill their fathers in order to sleep with their mothers at some point in their psychosexual development. Suppose that young kids indeed feel that their "all mighty" fathers are actually their competitors for the love and affection they get from their mothers—will it be healthy to live in close patriarchal cells led by the authority of such fathers, then?

The answer is probably not. But nuclear patriarchal cells of marriage where the mothers and the kids collected around the father, depended on the father, subjected themselves to the father, but, to a degree, also had their freedom ignored and their rights annulled by the father—were favored by society for most of human history. Living in such oppressive conditions might be way more tyrannical and damaging for children than trying to educate them to be self-restrained and civilized individuals—no matter what Freud might have said.

But while women's gatherer nature might be better fit for cultivating the nuclear family nest, men are total strangers to the concept of the nuclear family, that is, from a biological standpoint. By nature, men are not interested in living in one family cell for good. Rather, they are interested in catching new females for maximum copulations that will guarantee ultimate spreading of their genes on the planet. That's the way it goes in nature, and, instinctively, human males are nothing different. However, since humans are much more intelligent and more developed creatures than beasts, humans created the family, the society, the culture, the tradition, the state, and the law to keep track of men's behavior, and, specifically, to control their sexual and reproductive habits.

The problem is not the society or the culture or the government or the law, but typically, the social, cultural, political, legal and economic measures powerful men take to cope with the situation. The problem is not even the concept of the family itself, but the particular type of family they impose on us. The nature of this family, that is, monogamous, heterosexual, nuclear, patriarchal and oppressive, used in controlling women's and men's sexual choices, commitments, fertility and reproduction, abortions and adoptions—is the heart of this problem.

Apparently, the traditional patriarchal family is an unfit solution when it comes to regulating sexual habits, personal relationships, and marriages. It also fails to cope impartially, that is without underlying patriarchal interests, with parenthood matters, issues concerning children, and economic and social matters related to maintaining family where each of the spouses has equal obligations and equal rights. The marriage institution still favors men to women in the most egoistic manner. The failure of this institution has to do with its unnatural and artificial nature, as much as with its underlying political motives. To satisfy the sociocultural, economical, and political interests, the patriarchal institution goes through imposing on women a certain illusionary way of life, discriminating woman and invading their privacy.

On top of that, the patriarchal marriage is so asynchronous with our twenty-first century's pace, our demanding standard of living, the high-technology we use, the flat world we belong to—that despite all the relentless efforts to preserve the marital wreckage afloat—the patriarchal marriage is losing its ground as a robust pillar of civilization. Slowly but surely, the patriarchal marriage is crumbling apart, because no longer can it stand behind the "perfect family" ideal it created centuries back. The naive ideals of order, stability, security, love, and commitment that characterized the "perfect family" for centuries are melting down in front of our eyes like the arctic glaciers in response to global warming. Like in global warming, for the most part, the reason is destructive intervention of humans and artificial control of the natural resources. Unquestionably, poisonous materialistic motives related to the patriarchal powers of society, the governments, the states, the corporations, the military, the enforcement, and their sociocultural, scientific and legal weapons—have brought us to this boiling point.

THE MONOGAMY THAT RULES

Let's face it. The patriarchal family, the one of hierarchal structure, where men's authority is at the top, and the one of strictly monogamous relationships—is artificial and in many ways unnatural to humankind. This type of family emerged from interests and politics rather than from any inherent natural law. It has gained momentum in response to masculine social goals and has grown into the full-fledged institution we know today, regulated by governments and states. But not only is this structure artificial, but its creation by patriarchal society has made it particularly poisonous. The way that the patriarchal society intervenes in women's personal lives and the choices women make about their sexuality, fertility, and reproduction, and the way it imposes on women certain socially unequal roles within the family through marriage, are specifically inciting.

Although to a much lesser degree than in the ancient Roman family, where the father had legal permission to kill his wife and kids,[17] the patriarchal control of the modern family is still catastrophic today when it comes to women's sexuality and individual freedom. The patriarchal illusion lingers on today with all its fictitious ideals about the "perfect choice" women should make about their lives.

For instance, marriage continues to be idealized, romanticized, and praised in society for its alleged benefit or intrinsic quality: monogamy. Monogamy, remaining sexually exclusive to only one husband for life, the patriarchal legend goes, helps you develop the "self-control" needed for your health and wealth. Monogamous marriage “may be one of the foundations of Western civilization, and may explain why democratic ideals and notions of human rights first emerged as a Western phenomenon.”[17] Monogamy will bring you "love" and surely also happiness. The only problem is, it doesn't. It doesn't because exactly like patriarchal marriage, monogamy is at its last breath. And that happens because monogamy and men's sexual behavior in real life strongly disagree with each other; because monogamy does not fit into the postmodern lifestyle, and because monogamy cannot live side by side with technology, globalization, and our modern pace. Therefore, monogamy today, exactly like marriage, is crumbling apart with skyrocketing divorce rates in the U.S. and around the Western world.

The proponents of monogamy usually say that monogamy, when practiced, has the potential to decrease sexually transmitted diseases (through having sex with one partner only), and to diminish potential genetic defects (when children of the same polygamous father inadvertently have sex). Yet, the social monogamy in humans is a form of family organization. It is a sociocultural and political creation, a model for family structure, on the one hand, and a mating system, on the other.

However, looking at other references of monogamy in nature, the phenomena of social monogamy in animals is quite rare. Rather, most of the animals in nature either run polygamous sex lives, copulating with more than one mate, or have serial-monogamous sex lives, engaging in consecutive sexual relationships with different, but exclusive, breeding mates, every mating season.[19] Monogamy appears mostly in birds and in a small percent of mammals, too. But even those animals that are known to be purely monogamous by nature copulate occasionally, on the side, with other opposite sex mates in what is known as "extra pair copulations." In such a behavior they definitely resemble men.

Throughout a large part of human history, for instance, in ancient times, humans have been having polygamous relationships both with opposite-sex and same-sex partners. Thus in the same manner that monogamy is used as a model for arranging families, polygamy can be used, and, indeed in some places, it is the prevalent family arrangement.[20]

But, for better or worse, monogamy is the preferred structure by most human cultures. And that might be positive, as long as sexual monogamy is not imposed by those cultures—especially not through a marriage contract. Because when it comes to men's sexual behavior, remaining sexually exclusive to the women is an unrealistic restriction.[21] This is because men appear to be less monogamous than women. According to cross-cultural studies, more men than women around the world engage in extramarital sex.[22] And that is because the sexually monogamous contract of marriage, where "extra pair copulations" are usually triggers for divorce, is nothing but a joke.

The only purely natural components of the patriarchal family are the by-products of copulation and reproduction, namely children. However, these two exist in the natural world, notwithstanding monogamy or polygamy. Most families in nature are ephemeral at best, and exist only until the offsprings are capable to stand on their own feet and survive independently. From a biological standpoint, the more intelligent the species are, the longer their learning curves toward gaining survival skills would be, and so in the case of human beings, child rearing in a family nest would take longer.

While creating families for producing and rearing children is a natural choice for most humans, the nature of such families is not. And the roles assigned to each of the partners in marriage are definitely not natural choices, but social ones, that is, in most cases, patriarchal choices made by men. During most of human history, monogamous patriarchal families were the rule, thanks to the dominant part that men played in politics, society, and culture. Men's natural traits of competitiveness, aggression, oppression, and exploitation against women also helped them maintain their high ranking social status that allowed them to dictate the "right" social and sexual practices to others.

Other patriarchal family components, such as cohabitating in a single household and sharing an economy (managed by men,) are similarly ingredients created by society and annexed to the modern family roles. Additionally, religious sacraments, traditional rites, and legal commitments, which are also central to the family today, are far from being natural ingredients.

Bottom line: the nuclear, monogamous, heterosexual family structure, requisite for marriage, is mostly a social creation rather than natural one. Such a family structure is a construct of men, society, and culture as a means of sexual control, regulations of reproduction and child rearing, and social, economic, and political domination.

The heterosexual monogamy is currently the only marital structure. The U.S. Defense of Marriage Act (DOMA) law of 1996 defined marriage for federal purposes as "only a legal union between one man and one woman as husband and wife."[23] That is, in order to get married one has to be in a relationship with an opposite-sex partner, and marrying more than one opposite-sex partner at a time is not allowed. Hence, same-sex relationships and polygamous relationships are not recognized by the federal government for marriage purposes. While heterosexual monogamy is still the most popular choice by most people, it would be wrong to assume that the heterosexual, monogamous, and patriarchal family structure can fit everyone and serve the good, contentment, and happiness of all.

Our Western society is definitely not experienced enough with alternative family structures to ban such structures and strictly impose just one way of life as it does. And upon further reflection: Why should only one family structure be supported by law while other family structures, viewed as positive by many people, are ignored? Why only heterosexual monogamy? Why not give a chance to homosexual monogamy and support it by law? Why not recognize genetic monogamy, that is two single partners who have a child together as one family cell for the purposes of benefits and rights? Such alternative structures are the need of the hour, and the growing number of women and men who do not accept the heterosexual and patriarchal structure are living proof of this need. Why not, then, experiment with alternative structures, learn about their pros and cons, and later, protect the most successful ones by law?

Why? Again, the answer has to do with interests. While it is clear that alternative family structures can benefit large parts of society who don't fit naturally into the strict patriarchal framework, our masculine society keeps forcing the idea of heterosexual monogamous marriage on us. The patriarchal society ignores the fact that the vast majority of men who live by monogamy in patriarchal marriage would opt out of it the first moment they could. Undoubtedly, the issue is still a social taboo, and it is still politically incorrect to say it. But, hey, we all know that men are "polygamy-minded" creatures in the sense that they always search for new sexual mates and are always ready to have sex whenever and wherever they have a chance.

While some men can live in monogamous units for a short period of time, they definitely can't be locked there for good. Particularly for this reason the patriarchs came up with the idea of oppression and exploitation in marriage. To tackle the "prisoner feelings" such men might feel in their gut whenever they are locked in the prison cell of marriage, they finally managed to channel their rage on suppressing and exploiting the "weaker" parts of civilization. The logic for this might be the following one: If bound by the marriage contract, men cannot have sex with as many women as they might have wanted, reproduce joyfully, and have countless kids—why don't they just conquer and use power through invasion, oppression, and exploitation of women and kids, or perhaps through conquering nations and lands? Subduing the family to the state through the patriarch is part of this plot, and imperial oppressive behavior by patriarchal rulers might be the consequence.

THE PHILOSOPHY OF OPPRESSION

Ideas of oppressive behavior by men against the family were stressed by the revolutionary French philosophers Gilles Deleuze, Felix Guattari, and Michel Foucault, who blamed the family for being the "first cell of the Fascist society." Foucault explained how we face fascism in our everyday lives by drawing parallels with the contemporary patriarchal family. In the preface to Deleuze and Guattari's *Anti Oedipus* (1972), he wrote: "…the fascism that causes us to love power, to desire the very thing that dominates and exploits us…"[24] In such a family, the child grows up loving the father (the head of the family, the dominant figure, but also the tyrannical figure), the very person who oppresses him. This creates in the child's mind a natural affinity for power figures and a perverse pleasure of loving and being loved by them in return. This child, in all probabilities, would grow up to become a tyrannical figure himself—owner and protector of women and children, on the one hand, and suppressor of the family, on the other. When this type of family serves as a microcosm of the larger society, chances are that such a child will use individual, materialistic, political or militaristic means to suppress populations and achieve his goals. And so, governed by patriarchal interests, the family becomes a model for oppression of women, children, and populations.

Way before the French philosophers, the political patriarchy and patriarchal marriage had been criticized by other thinkers, among them John Locke (1632-1704) who believed that marriage should be voluntary, based on consent, and not on marital hierarchy or interest.[25] This contrasted the involuntary nature of marriage prevalent at Locke's time, and the fact that women had limited alternatives to choose from in the first place.

Another criticism came a century later from John Stuart Mill (1806-1873) who suggested that subordination of women to men in a hierarchy originated in physical force men exerted on women.[26] Indeed, during the coverture married women were deprived of legal rights and gained them only through their husbands. Mill compared women's conditions to sheer slavery, accentuating men's interest in retaining the slavery for their own good. Mill came against women discrimination and exploitation in depriving them of legal rights, exposing them to abuse, and imposing on them intimacy with their husbands; and even went further questioning the prevailing thought that women's nature "justified" patriarchal inequality in marriage. Mill concluded that the prevailing inequality in marriage is unjust, non-educational, and, thus has the ability to corrupt the future citizens, as equality was the cornerstone of just relationships and a pillar of a fair society, he believed.

Other philosophers who stressed the destructive power of patriarchal marriage in its use of force against women and exploitation of women were the Marxists. Friedrich Engels (1820-1895), for instance, believed that such a relationship has its roots in the defeat of the female sex to the patriarchal forces.[27] Engels suggested that patriarchal marriage was based on economic reasoning, whereby women were treated like private properties owned by men. Thus, he saw in patriarchal marriage a kind of victory of the "private property" over the more natural "communal property." In Engels' view, such a marriage allowed men to own women, control their reproduction, and enhance their private property through giving birth to their heirs.

In *The Communist Manifesto,* Karl Marx (1818-1883) claimed that women have turned into "instruments of production" for men and thus the private family should be abolished in order to liberate women from the patriarchal destructive and tyrannical control.[28]

Similarly, more modern thinkers accepted the idea that the patriarchal family arose from the development of private property and the consequent domination of women by men to stake their claims on that private property. The patriarchal family with a dominating father, according to such views, is a prototype of a state with an autocratic head. Thinkers such as the psychiatrist Wilhelm Reich (1897-1957), who influenced Michel Foucault and the French philosophers, contended that such sexually-suppressed patriarchal structures cultivates propertarian and authoritarian societies brimming with neuroses.[29] According to such a view, patriarchal and monogamous marriage is compulsive and appears to be nothing but a euphemism for the domineering male with subordinate dependents and, at large, a model for a sick state.

THE ILLUSION BLOWS UP IN OUR FACE

History shows that the patriarchal marriage owes nothing to natural preferences, to equality between the genders, to pure friendship or even to "love." Throughout history, social and economic considerations were the most salient considerations taken into account in marital commitments. Even at our postmodern age, along with its global economic integration, advanced technology, and women's liberation, basing relationships solely on romantic "love" is not really serious.

It is true that today gender equality, friendship, and more individualism have come into play, but still, whoever tells you she decided to marry only because she was "crazy in love" with her guy is probably fooling you. Not only because "love" never existed in the first place or because "love" was invented by humans to justify their choices to have convenient sex, but also because capitalism and interests do go hand in hand, and in a very materialistic manner. After all, you can't turn a blind eye to the fact that while the poor dream to marry the rich and usually fail in their mission, the rich keep marrying the rich to preserve their familial wealth and social prestige. Many couples keep marrying for social, economic, and political interests, exactly like in the past centuries, if not even more, while others discern the illusion behind this fake institution.

No matter if you believe in natural "love" or think that "love" is a social phenomenon or a humankind invention—the truth of the matter is that social, political, and economic interests have driven Western society to support patriarchal marriage and not any magical potion of “love.” This type of marriage flourished at the expense of natural sexual choices and at the expense of fruitful companionships and true friendships. The sad part about the patriarchal marriage is that it has always been an illusion, a cover-up for the underlying motives; a perfect make-believe that generation after generation has learnt to accept. Like the heroine Anna said in Leo Tolstoy's timeless novel *Anna Karenina* before putting an end to her miserable marital life: marriage is a lie, it's a cover-up for human animosity. But throughout human history, it was natural to get married, it was healthy, it was right, good, and beautiful, and divine, while no one really posed the question: why?

Like a sedative drug, society injected this patriarchal illusion religiously into the cultural veins and fed it through the cultural pipelines: From traditional gender roles nurtured at home, through socialization of kindergarten girls playing with Barbie dolls, to school education teaching kids to accept gender inequality with more scientific subjects for boys and more humanitarian subjects for girls. The society continued to inject discriminating rules at work, endow the family benefits to the "patriarchally-married" couples only, and impose religious rites.

The social pressure was propagated by the media, through the visual arts, the cinema, the theater, and the learnt academia, to name a few—all of which worked in concert to embellish marriage and create an ideal picture in the minds of millions. But at the same time, these ideals intentionally benefited the patriarchal institutions themselves. Few were the thinkers who questioned the patriarchal marriage for real, and so this illusion was among the most successful illusions ever. It became socially right and also trendy to tie the knot. Everybody dreamed of a big wedding, no matter how expensive it was, all through the later part of the twentieth century. And yes, it was also a useless thing to drive a wedge in the fundamentals of this institution, for too many patriarchal forces were interested in its eternal growth. No governing patriarchs of society were willing to question the prevalent authority, and, as a matter of fact, it's quite understandable why.

Now fast forward to the twenty first century. It is amazing to see what has happened to the patriarchal family. It has exhausted itself, and now it is melting away in front if our eyes. First and foremost because relationships, commitments, and family matters cannot be determined by the same guidelines, gender biases, and laws governing the past generations. Similarly because the illusion of the patriarchal institution—the one that sees the nuclear monogamous family as a precondition to health and wealth, social order, security and stability, love and happiness for the individual, the family, the nation, and the entire universe— has lost its ground.

The patriarchal marriage has exhausted itself.

Women's roles in our society have changed tremendously in the past centuries, from assuming solely the caretaker roles in the family to becoming equal breadwinners; from fully submitting themselves to men's authority to becoming erudite, self-sufficient, and financially independent of men. Likewise, times have changed, and new industrial and technological means have emerged, transportation and communication technologies improved, and the media gained substantial power. The computerization and digitization of many aspects of our lives and the Internet revolution gave further rise to alternative ideas, relationships, as well as alternative family structures such as the single parent family and the homosexual family.

All the more, the grand improvements in our quality of life, along with longevity, higher standard of living, globalization, and economic prosperity, have all put individualistic and the hedonistic interests in the forefront. This came at the expense of the social interests, making the sacrifice "for the sake of the family" a less desired option today. Our mindset has changed greatly from restricting ourselves to just a few options, to virtually facing endless alternatives to get to know people, create social connections, cooperate in various physical and virtual spaces, study and work together, cohabitate, have sex, start up families, have kids or make abortions, adopt kids, and use surrogates, to name a few.

Evidently, in such a cultural climate, the patriarchal family can no longer deliver the goods. A monogamous, nuclear, and patriarchal family should no longer be a prior condition for living together or sharing economy, for having sex, or even for having and raising kids. We have reached an epoch where marriage and parenthood should be separated from one another. Clearly at our time, endowment of social and government rights to couples must be separated from legal patriarchal constrains.

Even the most conservative traditional marriage proponents today slowly wake up from the ideal marriage dream. More and more open-minded people today are unafraid to look at the truth, get more realistic about marriage, and skeptical as well. Indeed, it is encouraging to see that this trend is becoming even more influential among the variety of less mediated and less tendentious community forums, social networks, and the blooming blogosphere on the web. We can now, more than ever, look at the patriarchal marriage with open eyes rather than through rose-tinted glasses.

4

Between Friendship and Wedlock

INDIVIDUALISTIC WINDS

"Marriage is dying!" said the young blonde to her friend checking out lingerie at the local Victoria Secret store. I certainly didn't mean to eavesdrop but, hey, I just couldn't help it....

Stuck in an unhappy marriage, the blonde felt she had lost her husband, who used to be her lover and her best friend—"just because he started up a new online business" and had no time for her. Looks like she wanted the good ole days back.

But the question is whether it makes sense. After all, one can't turn a blind eye to the fact that something has happened to friendships today, including intimate friendships in marriage. New types of friendships have emerged. And these new friendships affected the institution of marriage whether we want to admit it or not.

When the blonde's husband started up an online business, this "digital extension" of himself invaded his personal life, and later, destroyed his relationship with his wife and ended their marriage. He became unfriendly with her and ignorant to her feelings. With every new online transaction he made came a deeper addiction to the "online dollar mill." He was dependent on his computers and tech gadgets, betrothed to his money, and servant to his virtual clients and friends.

He preferred to be part of various online spaces, forums, and business communities to communicating with his wife directly, face to face. He preferred clients to friends, work to home, and his looming business to any interactions with his wife. But at the point where his online transactions transcended his physical relations, his wife noticed a big change. Not only did not they have sex anymore, but they were no longer friends. For her, it was friendship where it began and friendship where it all ends.

One reason for the demise of friendship has to do with our electronic age—modern technology, the online super fast flow of information, instant communication, and the instant gratification that follows. Speedy interactions and the immediate feedback people, employers, and friends demand from us daily have changed the way we live and think today. Any clear cut boundaries between the personal and public domains have been also wiped away, as work and home now dance a very intimate techno tango. The beat is kept fast and spontaneous in many ways, but, at the same time, addicting and demanding round the clock participation. Our physical space and our individual freedom have certainly been affected, despite the fact that we live in the most independent and liberated age.

The question that needs to be asked here is: What

happened to our friendships today and how they changed our attitude toward marriage. How was marriage affected by the new kinds of friendships that emerged?

Apparently, today, more than in the past, many couples create bonds, partnerships, and also marriages due to "friendships," to later find themselves, usually after a couple of years, breaking up or divorcing due to lack of "friendship." The rise of friendship and its death, like the rise of marriage and its death, have to do with the growth of our commercial society. The modern capitalism we live by, the global economic integration, and the relative financial prosperity, at the international, national, and the interpersonal levels—all allowed for more disposable income. And more income means more financial independence, and with regards to women, an enhanced dependence on the self rather than on men.

According to the American historian Carl Degler, the rise of individualism can date back to the Enlightenment movement in the eighteenth century.[1] The logic and reason that characterized the philosophy of the Enlightenment have set new rules and, coupled with the Industrial Revolution's mechanization and automation taking place in the later part of the same century, the power of individualism grew even further. The enormous scientific and technological innovations that came after the Industrial Revolution, with better means of transportation, communication, and aviation technologies, and, later, the outburst of computation, culminating in the Internet revolution of the twentieth century—have all accelerated the individualistic trend, making it the centerpiece of modern civilization. Technological advancement also played a key role in scientific and medical breakthroughs, which in turn extended our life expectancy and improved our standard of living—propping up individualism to a greater extent.

Beyond theory, in practice, individualism was first and foremost a new state of mind. From the age of the Enlightenment onward, this individualistic mindset culminated in the 1960s with the civil rights movement fighting against racial discrimination and the feministic movement advocating for equal rights for women, both gaining extraordinary momentum.

Thanks to feministic activists women's rights were changed forever, making women equal individuals before the law with equal rights for education, suffrage, work, and sexual liberties. Women's emancipation and liberation movements vitalized the prevailing individualistic forces within the modern society. No longer were female individuals physically, emotionally, and economically dependent on men—but more and more of them were self-reliant and made their voices heard in the workplace, in academia, in business, in politics, and through social and cultural participation.

Individualism entailed importance of key values such as independence, financial freedom, and freedom of choice to western society. And so the individual, rather than the family, the nation, or the state, became the key player. Everything revolved around the individual and her free choices, including her goals, her career, her business, her home, her family, her entertainment, and also her friends.

SOME FRIENDLY DIVERSIONS

But what kind of friends have we become when most of our connections have turned impersonal, virtual, and almost completely unreal? When we take part in countless online forums, virtual nets, and social communities anonymously or with thousands of online "friends"? When we are subscribed to an endless number of messages and tweets every day that come from everywhere? When photos and videos are streamed to us directly, through our portable devices, through our emails and endless SMS? Who is delivering this information? Our bosses? Our colleagues? Our family? Our friends? Everyone or no one at all? Are these friendships real or just virtual reflections of the postmodern generation?

In a sense, everyone is now friends with everyone, virtually everyone, that is. But what about real friendships? The absurd thing about friendships now is that while the friendship mode is "enabled" at its most basic level, meaning that, theoretically, an infrastructure exists with an ability to become friends with everyone—in reality, there are very limited people who can be called "true friends."

Nonetheless, some people take pride in their hundreds, or even thousands, of Facebook connections, as if they were real friends. Some of those connections were real friends somewhere in their past. Others can be mere strangers, John Does at best and online products or services, at the worst. But they are now all connected and share their personal stories. They send their photos, tag their names, and notify of updates in their virtual statuses. They vote in "likes" and "dislikes" about their "friends" and also do it repetitively, almost robotically, several times a day. No matter who invited those folks to send those messages, fact is that most people on those social nets will accept a "virtual flower" or a "virtual kiss" even when it comes from a complete stranger.

While Facebook and similar media might be seen as nothing but pointless distractions from daily routine, most people relish the mindless disruption. Some even like this amusing game with connection to avatars and "simulacra of friends." Others might be too busy or too lazy to even think about this new friendly phenomenon that has engulfed the digital world. Either way, priorities have changed in our digital age. While connections in real life with real people about daily issues are considered boring "time wasters"—the real time wasters in life have captured people's attention, time, and energy in an unprecedented way. It is unbelievable to see how so many mature adults still find enough time to spend on those online replicas they now call "friends."

Living in the postmodern age, people's lives have changed tremendously. People spend less and less time on casual "unimportant" routines and interactions. They believe that avoiding the mundane things of life will free their minds and allow them more time for the "real interactions". Most people don't need to know the owner of their grocery store or the person who grows the vegetables they buy. These folks, who were part of people's lives in past centuries, have nothing to do with people's lives today. People don't need to know their neighbors, because neighbors come and neighbors go. And some couples don't even care about their child's school teacher, as long as he's checking his homework and does not complain about the boy.

And the same applies to the virtual spaces—people

don't really want to know all those avatars, icons, images, friends, and friends of friends in reality. They are just amusing distractions, short and entertaining comic relief from their busy daily tasks. They don't know who John Doe is, what he's doing in Japan, and why in the world he's raising an Iguana with his girlfriend. Thinking of it, they have never spoken to John. But just in case, they keep him on their list. The new digital culture makes them believe that this kind of friendship is trendy and hip, and it may add something extra to who they are or think they are.

Similar impersonal, almost anonymous relationships, products of the capitalistic system, commercial society, and industrialization were believed to be the interactions that have the power to enhance personal self-interest, competitiveness, and people's ability to create significant personal relationships or true friendships. That is, through turning the economic relations (e.g., relations with different sellers of products and services) to impersonal relations—the personal relations, in turn, could morph into more significant relations based on friendliness and affection and affinity. Such an idea was held by the liberal economist Adam Smith (1723-1790)[2] who believed that capitalism would set people free to create true relationships based on who people really like, and not perfunctory commercial relationships.

A few centuries ahead, in our digital age, indeed people have choice. Plenty of choice, actually. Most of the individuals living today in the western capitalistic and democratic states clearly support freedom and personal choice in everything, including in their friendships, relationships, and marriages.

But what kind of choices are they? Are they affinity based? Are they interest free? Due to the immense pressures postmodern individuals face in their hectic lives, most of them look for distractions and amusements from their tedious daily routines, both at work and at home. And due to men's playful nature, the need for such entertaining distractions applies more to men's psyche than to women's psyche. Such relief can be found abundantly on virtual community networks, in various online forums, message boards, games, and other online platforms. Interactions over such social media are usually characterized by elements of playfulness, rather than by seriousness, by impermanence rather than by stability, and by chance rather than by order, logic, and reason.

The user-friendly look and feel of such virtual platforms is also light and entertaining in essence. Such user interfaces consist of colorful images, and distracting videos in addition to text carrying some information, if any at all.

Other "friendly" networks are established for the purpose of product or service marketing, for nothing but promotional campaigns. In such a case, certain key players in the company usually post their merchandise, their products or services through the virtual social nets to all their listed "friends."

Other threads are carefully crafted for self-marketing, for building a serious or trustworthy online persona, for promoting personal or corporate identity to businesses, organizations, or corporations. Of course, such friendly images have nothing to do with true identities or real-life relationships. Such personas are essentially avatars, replicas, and simulacra of "friends," which are designed to amuse men or sell things to them, or both to amuse and to sell. But this way of adding people's names to a network of "friends" in order to promote products or services or sell them in action is now considered "all the rage."

The methods used to maintain these "friendship" sites are also unnatural, unserious, and essentially fake. Most images, texts, and sounds are carefully doctored to entertain or to market unrealistic perfect images. Most texts, images, videos, and sounds are reproduced, retouched, remixed and matched to make users feel they really like this new "user-experience": the friendly design, the cool sound, the smashing look and feel—in other words, the goods being sold. Through this commercial affinity, the capitalists convince adult women and men they really belong to a great "community of friends," to "followers," to "smart users," to "fans".

But such crafty methods where friendship is harnessed to business are nothing but traps that make people waste their money and swipe their credit cards. Usually that's all there is to these virtual friendships.

Similarly to commercial products or services, postmodern friendships have become artificial, commercialized, expertly designed, improved, talked back, interlinked and optimized skillfully. On various web-pages, blogs, and virtual communities—such friendships are now tracked by Google and other search engines and come up at the top of the search. The improved ranking of such fake friendships can lead to better targeting, to more revenues and return on investment for the sponsors.

But, at the end of the day, one asks herself what the buzz is all about. Is it all for real? Real people? Real relationships? True value friends? Or just a well marketed techno bubble, a friendly diversion at best, and a boggling nonsense, at worst. You really needn't be a Nobel Prize nominee to realize how the perception of friendship has gone bankrupt these days. Men either turned their friendship into a mere distraction, for the purpose of entertainment, amusement or fun. Or, they sold their friendship to the devil, commercializing it exactly like other products or services on the net. Men often find themselves consuming those "friendships" as if they were magic pills. They hope they will make them feel better, more belonging, and emotionally strong. But, the more they consume this online pill, the less connected to reality they get.

Most men have plenty of choices to make and plenty of potential friends and female mates, but at the end of the day they are left bewildered. Their choices, too, are occasionally shaky, flimsy, based on seizing the moment instead of forethought for future plans. In the same manner, the corresponding friendships, relationships, and marriages are nothing but unstable.

This has to do with the unlimited opportunities men face daily, the playful atmosphere, and the new virtual spaces that emerged. No longer is friendship precious, special, and won through pain, sweat and perseverance, for instance, like the ancient platonic friendships among men. This original kind of friendship cannot exist in societies where commercial and political interests overpower relationships among real people.

Friendships today, more and more, look like pure economical transactions. They are hit products with millions of "click-throughs" a day. Friendships are cheaper than a bottle of soda. They are highly accessible and come in huge volumes and replicas. Yet, those friendships are frail, for they are intended to satisfy interests of the self in the most hedonistic measures.

Postmodern men are now slaves to entertainment, to excitement and pleasure, to indulging sex and passion, and to money in the most extreme way. In this greedy world, the men's satisfaction and egoistic goals outweigh public goals and common interests. In such a selfish climate, relationships and marriages based on true friendships—that is, sensitive, compassionate, and cooperating ones—cannot live. Like dominoes, they fall apart, for they have lost their relevance.

WHEN FRIENDSHIP & INTEREST CONVERGE

Most individuals nowadays are presented with an unimaginable number of "virtual friends" to pick from. Most citizens of the global world have endless opportunities to socialize, intermingle, and get to know people from different backgrounds, cultures, and states. The world became flat, and people don't really have to be physically present in order to connect, both in business and at home.[3] Telecommunications services have grown exponentially. And now, plentiful wireless laptops, iPads, and super speedy smart phones with webcams and voice capacities connect people. With full-fledged Internet, email, and SMS services working on wireless platforms through speed of light web connections, using instant messengers, and Internet call services—citizens of the global world have become the kings of communication and the lords of information.

Everyone and everything is within their reach as they experiment with new adventures and conquer new domains each and every day. But since virtually anyone can be friends with everyone at the click of a button today, the choices have become less and less dependent on the value of true friendship, particularly for men.

The new friendships have long lost their virginity. They have morphed into something else: into amusing interactions, pleasant distractions, pure monetary transactions, commercial ads, sheer interest-driven short romances, or unemotional steamy sex.

The economic power of the Western world has increased immensely, along with its technological control and its sociocultural and political dominance in the global world. The true value of friendship has been changed. And such a political, social, and economic domination of our world has clearly assisted in propelling autonomic desires, individualistic whims, selfishness, and possessiveness.

Today, more than in the past, friendships hinge on interests. Be they social, political, economic, or mere physical and sexual. Various interests come between the real "hunches" and the expected personal gain from these "hunches." In today's capitalistic world, where time amounts to lots of money, people tend to weigh out meticulously every single bit of their interactions, factoring in personal gain. Perhaps it is an un-politically-correct assertion, but friendship, like marriage, is smitten with egoistic desires and governed colossally by materialistic interests which are now key components of our capitalistic age.

However this close connection between friendships and interests, particularly men's interests, is nothing new. Past generations, too, had their interests meshed with their relationship choices in one way or another. History shows that when it comes to marriages, relationships, and friendships, choices were never immaculate or interest free. Only before the Neolithic revolution of the Stone Age, relatively friendly and egalitarian hunter-gatherer societies existed, where men mostly hunted and women mostly gathered food.[4] Such societies lived in bands and tribes, and, due to their nomadic lifestyles, they did not accumulate or move their possessions. So, naturally, no hierarchal organization was established, yet.[5]

Later, with the move to agrarian and domesticated lifestyles, following the Neolithic revolution, new interests came into play: Apart from the basic food provision (through hunting and gathering, fishing, and agriculture), reproduction, and raising the kids—ownership of farmsteads and lands became important, too. From this point onward, companionships gradually lost their "innocence" and focused on interest—on growing food, and, later in the Bronze Age, also on breeding, trading crafts and goods, and owning lands. During these prehistoric periods, before record history, friendships started to be used for attaining material targets. Apparently, friendships, marriages and interests began their close ties at a very early stage.

Much later, in the patriarchal societies of the ancient times, where the obedience of wives to their husbands and oppression of women and kids became the standard rule—what kind of friendship among couples could one expect? Friendship based on affection and affinity did not exist in Pater (father based or patriarchal), hierarchy-based families, such as the Roman families, which included everyone, even the slaves, under the authority of the father in the household. In such societies, the roles of women were clear: to give birth to kids, raise them, and serve the kids and their husbands relentlessly, while their husbands often led polygamous relations with their concubines.[6] What kind of true friendship among couples could one expect?

However, at the same time, among men, brave friendships did prevail. Those were strong, faithful, and extremely passionate relationships, based on loyalty and complete devotion to the friend. They were close friendly ties, intimate at times, and targeted at the pursuit of ideals and virtues. No family interactions between a husband and a wife or even between a parent and a child could amount to such spiritual and lofty friendships. Such strong friendships were pretty rare, though.

In the medieval period, the morality and the search for good among friends were replaced by social and economic interests. Materialistic aspects came into play, whenever friends were obliged to help their friends financially. Landlords and vassals had their feudal relationship fixed in fealty oaths,[7] and the privileged classes usually used their friendships and marriages as an effective means of climbing the social ladder. The friendships, the kinships, and the marriages were excellent tools to promote the social status, to protect the current holdings of a family, to increase the family fortune, and to extend political impact.

During the Renaissance, from the fourteenth

through the middle of the seventeenth century, the classical idealistic friendship made a comeback in the culture in the form of great humanistic and aesthetical and literary ideals.[8] Although this trend persisted through the eighteenth and nineteenth centuries, for the most part, friendship was idealized. The real relationships and marriages based on “love at first sight” were regarded foolish, crazy, or even tragic and fatal. A well-known example is Shakespeare's tragedy *Romeo and Juliet* (1595) depicting "mad love" between two youngsters and their rival families which disallow their romance.[9] The story culminates in the tragic death of both lovers to the astonished eyes of the feuding sides. Evidently, at these times of growing urbanization, commerce and trade[10] interests continued to play a role in creating bonds of friendships and marriages.

The interest component, particularly interest of men, continued to be the most salient feature in relationships and marriages through the later part of the eighteenth century. The Industrial Revolution introduced change to individual familial responsibilities but did not change the basic division of roles that continued to be gendered. In the aftermath of the Industrial Revolution, men ventured out to work in the emerging factories in industrialized cities, and the responsibilities for kids' education, healthcare, and welfare of the family, previously taken care of by the women within the family nest, gradually passed to public institutions and the states.

However, this did not affect women's discrimination and the fact women were nothing but servants to their men rather than their friends. As long as women adhered to the gender roles and depended on men financially—relationships were illusive: on the one hand perfectly courteous and friendly to the outside world, on the other, oppressive, exploitative, and abusive. Women were still discriminated against, as strict gender roles still defined work for women at home with caretaking and the household, and work for men in the factories and corporations.

In the eighteenth century married women could not work outside the home, could not study, could not vote, and had no legal rights before the law. All the more, women had no rights to decide about their own sexual matters—so true companionships and marriages based on real friendships, that is, egalitarian ones of equal rights, trust, and mutual respect were not seen on the horizon then.

With the rise of the Romantic Movement in the second half of the eighteenth century, an intellectual movement that stressed individual's emotions rather than pure reason of the cold industrial age—more sensible or friendly treatment of women appeared mainly in the art and in the literature.[11] But no dramatic shift appeared in the division of labor between women and men, and women rights did not revolutionize during that time. Thus friendly relations, in fact existed, but always with respect to the strict gender roles defined by men.

Evidently, the move to industrialized society, urbanization, the anonymity of the big city, and the continued emergence of a commercial society with the high production and consumption it entails—have all strengthened the value of individualism in relationships. Later, the rise of technology that persisted through the twentieth century, and continues to progress, also supported the individuality seed within relationships, but mostly that of men.

Men were still much freer as individuals to do what they wanted outside the home and outside of marriage, too, where their places at home as the prime breadwinners and decision makers were secured. Through submission of the wife and the kids to their authority at home, men still had the upper hand. For instance, no real friendship could exist in the Victorian double-faced society, in the nineteenth century where women where completely subsumed by men.

Later, in the twentieth century, features such as spacious homes decorated with beautiful gardens, motor vehicles, and new electrical appliances (mainly in the fifties)—did not really create true friendly conditions for families, but rather sold sanctimonious and embellished ideals to the masses. Most relationships at these times still centered on interest, on men exploiting women, and on political, social, and financial profit.

Although the standard of living had surely risen by the middle of the twentieth century, most women still carried on with their traditional gender roles. Women were not self-sufficient, and they depended on their men financially. Women were still not free to take their own independent paths in life with regard to their body, sexuality, and fertility matters.

In the fifties, the states and the emerging corporations still continued to communicate the same American dream messages to the public through all available media. That patriarchal message aimed to justify and preserve the men's superiority within society and culture. Conjugal harmony based on such patriarchal "friendships" continued until the bubble exploded in the sixties with the advent of the pill and the women liberation movements that advocated for more rights for women (in addition to the rights of equal education, work and vote which were already granted).

From the sixties onward, with equal rights before the law and with equal powers to take responsibility of their own sexuality, women felt freer than ever to put an end to the phony patriarchal "friendships."

In the twenty-first century, freedom of choice has become the cornerstone of modern civilization. This freedom has become crucial to friendships, relationships, and marital decisions as well. However, the difference now is that women, not only men, can pull the strings, define and redefine their friendships.

Women are now freer than ever to select their partners, their lovers, and their friends. Furthermore, more and more women today take an active part in politics and public opinion, in the academia, in science, in technology, in the arts, and in business. Many women maintain successful careers in parallel to their busy roles as mothers. And a growing number of women are financially independent of men.

More and more women play with men on equal grounds today. And precisely this equal position, coupled with women's rising financial liberty, has given further rise to women's individualistic interests in their relationships and to their ability to actually attain them. The rise of friendships based on romantic "love" and fulfilling relationships based on physical and emotional compatibility where women are dominant, not only men, are the direct result of this sweeping liberalization trend.

FRIENDSHIP INSIDE OUT: THE SEXY SIDE

Today, at the start of the twenty-first century, more and more women are continually equating their status to the status of men. The current statistics show that women surpassed men and now comprise over 50 percent of the workforce in the U.S.[12] This has happened for the first time in the nation's history. Statistics show that four out of ten mothers are the primary breadwinners in American families. And the recent global economic crisis (of 2008-2010) well intensified this trend. Women today drive education and business forward. They earn sixty percent of the college degrees awarded each year in the U.S. and fully half of the professional degrees and the PhDs. Almost forty percent of the working women today hold managerial positions in business. And in eighty percent of families, it is the women who make the buying decisions rather than the men.

Today, women take active parts in science and technology, in academia, in politics and in law. Women shine as intellectuals and succeed in various cultural and artful activities: as journalists, actresses, players, singers, dancers, and in various fields of sports. No longer are women confined to pink collar occupations, such as secretaries, typists, clerks and kindergarten teachers—like they used to be in the first half of the twentieth century. At the start of women's emancipation process such jobs only stressed women's inequality and inferiority against men's prestigious careers.

Today, women's decision making positions in society and their roles in the free market have empowered women's financial, mental, and physical freedoms. But, above all, it is a transformation in the mindset of women which has allowed for this change and not just external sociocultural effects. Women's psych has changed completely. More and more women are confident in their capabilities to get around in today's world without being reliant on men. Women now are freer individuals to make their own choices and no man on the planet can really stand in their way.

One of the top decisions women make today concerns their friendships, relationships, and marriages. Thanks to women's liberation and the change in the cultural mindset— women are now freer than ever to select their mates. Over ninety percent of the women interviewed for my book stated that they select their "boy-friends," based on their common values and not just on affection and affinity. The top value is definitely strong friendships, followed by compassion, successful communication, integrity, mutual respect, intellectual compatibility, sophistication and humor, and lastly, physical compatibility, or "romantic love," which is nothing but a euphemism for "sex."

And, speaking of sex, the interviews clearly show that today's women are certainly interested in intimate compatibility with their partners. They look for exciting lovers and fulfilling relationships that "create sparks" rather than boring or routine sex lives. Most women are also interested in building long-term relationships that can last and culminate in the creation of a family in the future, although not necessarily though a traditional marriage contract, as more and more women today elect to be singles. Most women also see their sexual relationships with their men as a significant act of "love" and as complimentary to their main goal: finding their "soul mate" and being the men's "best friends."

Grounding relationships on "true friendships" or being the men's "best friend" is certainly great progress in women's decision making pattern compared to the past generations. In was just a century back when women were selected based on their sexual attractiveness and their ability to provide good care-taking services to children and men. Social and political reasons also played roles then, when men married to promote their social and political ranks in the family and women married up wealthy men.

But since most women are educated and liberated today, participate equally in the workplace and are self-sufficient—women "erase" the traditional gender gaps in many ways. Postmodern women's higher financial status, and the greater self-esteem that comes with that, allows women to raise their expectations of their partners and look for additional added values such as intellect, good communication, a sense of humor, integrity, and mutual respect.

Another postmodern phenomenon highly regarded today is sexual compatibly. Having rocking sex lives with men and creating "orgasmic bliss" in bed is definitely of precious value. But most of my interviewees agreed that sex alone is too feeble a component to base the relationship upon. "It must come with great communication, admiration, and lots of respect on both sides." women said. All the interviewees agreed unanimously that partners should be basically equal in their give and take in relationships today.

"No side should feel inferior, and both sides must work in concert." Lauren, a twenty-nine year old violinist said. She explained to me that for her to consider someone a "lover," he must first be her "best friend." "There is no other way" she said decisively, referring to the affectionate conversations she had with her partner, Tom, who, like her, is a professional musician. Lauren was "in love" with Tom, because he was her "soul mate," first and foremost, her "best friend," and only later, her lover. She shared with me how they used to talk for hours about philosophy, art, and music, all their mutual interests, before they had sex. She also made her point clear about intelligence, saying that whenever intellectual compatibility is not there, friendships won't work for her. She spoke of their "mutual work on the relationship" and the compromises they both had to make in order to fuel the friendship fire time and time again. "Friendship is like a concert where each partner must know his part very well." She said metaphorically. "You definitely need to know your part and practice it a lot for the music to sound great in the live concert."

But let's not be naïve. Such relationship concerts will most likely sound harmoniously when the partner is financially stable, professionally successful, and, economically speaking, does well. In Lauren's case, Tom was a nice Jewish guy who came from a very wealthy New York family. I bet this fact did not interfere with Lauren's ultimate decision to pick him as her "best friend."

Because it's such a delicate issue and surely a social taboo to even mention financial interests in relation to selecting a "friend"—fifty percent of the women I interviewed denied this fact outright, sanctimoniously mentioning they did not care about the guy's financial status. But another significant fifty percent of the women gave me their candid take. They said that affluent guys would be much better candidates as partners. Such guys, they believed, might be better equipped to face the reality, and less likely to harbor fear of powerful women, if the men themselves were professionally successful in their own right and financially self-made.

I must admit that the high percentage of women who factored in the financial status of men did not take me by surprise; despite the fact most of the women who participated in my interviews were self-sufficient and independent.

Why should self-made women living in today's capitalistic world be interested in wealthy men? Turns out that money is still wrapped up in self-esteem for many women, exactly like it used to be in the past, if not more so today.

But, unlike in the past, where women fully depended upon men, women today are financially independent. And, precisely because of that, most of them said they are after financial compatibility with their men, to avoid financial dependence on them from the side of the men. But other women believe that their quest for a wealthy man is like a sticky complex inherited to women by past generations, by women who were dependent on men financially, by women who had no other choice to get around in their lives than to rely on the men.

It could certainly be so. It could also be a modern phenomenon, a trendy requirement of our capitalistic environment. It appears that in our materialistic society, women always strive to choose the best of the best partners they can get, and the most compatible ones with regards to financial and sociocultural aspects.

All of my interviewees regarded working as a team as a crucial element for their partnership's success. Such teamwork begins with being "soul mates" for each other and also sharing compassion, mutual dignity, and mutual respect. Being compatible intellectually and sharing communication skills, humor, and, of course, the aforementioned sex are also of significant importance.

The financial status of the guy was significant and factored in, because, apparently, partnerships are still economic transactions. When friendships today are almost traded in the stock exchange market, money has become an indispensable part of every decision people make, including the ones about their relationships and friendships. Essentially this is why, in our postmodern age, self-sufficient women still consider the aspect of financial compatibility.

But due to women's financial independence—it is from a starting point of strength, power, and freedom of choice that financial compatibility in men is sought not from a position of inferiority or weakness like in the past generations.

A Friendly Wakeup Call

Women are presented today with countless virtual and real alternatives and nice guys to pick from. But often the male supply exceeds the demand, because, due to the less monogamous nature of men, they are essentially unserious in their relationships with women and actually able to play simultaneously with more than one woman at a time. So, smartly enough, women today learned to take their own precautions against such misconducts through placing a higher value on themselves as mates.

It is not only our capitalistic world that makes women want to pick up financially compatible successful men. And it is not just complexes women carry on their backs from past generations. It is also the innermost nature of men and the awkward manner they make their decisions about women. Stripping women in their heads, men always look first at the sexual attractiveness of women and weigh their potential to get them laid. It is only later that they start their "friendly" games.

Unlike women, who like to be loved romantically in bed, who look at sex as a bonus to the friendships they have, and look at men as their perfect "soul mates" and their compassionate friends, men are after one thing, spelled S-E-X! Sex and only sex is what keeps them ticking and sticking to the same woman for a period of time that usually amounts to a couple of years, at best. Due to their competitiveness, aggression, and their hormonal structure, men are interested in the best sexual prey they can get. And they make their decisions about this prey through physical interactions mostly.

When men see a sexy woman, they literally stop thinking and focus instinctively on impressing her with their manliness. As we have already learned, women interfere with their line of thought.[13] From time immemorial, men have been diligent hunters, interested more in the process of catching their prey than in the destination, pleasurable intercourse with their prey. But as soon as their prey is captured and they get the woman laid, they gradually lose their interest in that woman and begin to look for the next.

Hard fact is that men love hunting games and will do just everything to get women laid; women they find physically attractive and sexually available. Unlike women, men are always sexually available, because, biologically speaking; they are designed to spread their genes on earth. Women, on the other hand, are less sexually available, because, emotionally, they get attached to their men.

Women are more after genuine friendships and, unlike men, they look for "soul mates" and egalitarian and respecting communications, because they are interested in creating warm nests. But men are afraid to be trapped in one nest. Plenty of nests will do the trick for them. And like "extra copulating" birds, men, too, occasionally spread their wings on the lookout for the next woman willing to spread her legs for them.

Thus the natural mindset of men is that of wanderers, of capricious and unstable players of games. For that reason, the postmodern "user-friendliness" phenomenon of plenty friendly interactions on virtual platforms and social nets—serves the interests of men more than the interests of women.

Contrary to men, women's mindset is that of nesters, more attached to a single space, both virtual and real space. Thus, the women's and the men's psyche stand in contradiction to one another, especially today, when men take advantage of the virtual nets.

On the other hand, women's roles have extended themselves beyond the traditional gender roles. Hence men should not confine women to their patriarchal order—as much as women should never trap men in one nest, for it's against men's biological nature. It would therefore be wise to be aware of this nature of men and take the right safety measures.

Let's face it. Men and friendships are not good friends, but men and sex are perfect soul mates! The problem is that women are still stuck somewhere down in the "soul mate" stage. It is surely a false perception, and something must be done about it here and now.

Here is a wake-up call. How can men be women's "best friends" and "soul mates" if they are constantly on the prowl for exciting sexual adventures? How can these men have egalitarian relationships with their women and provide them mutual respect while crossing and double crossing the lines time after time?

How can horny men be stuck in a marital cage without playing their physical and virtual games? Statistics show that infidelity in men is a much higher probability than in women. Men are greater cheaters and more unfaithful to their spouses than women.[14] However, due to their multitude of roles, at work and home with kids, women sometimes neglect this fact and settle down for miserable relationships with stable, yet, treacherous, men—relationships where jealousy and hatred play major roles.

Women must definitely do their best to avoid such grave mistakes by never committing in the first place.

Black on white: women can't be blind. Men are absolutely unreliable creatures when it comes to marriages, relationships, and friendships. And that absolutely gives legitimacy to independent women to be with men on the same page.

The logic works like this: if men pick women based on their physical attractiveness—why don't women consider men based on the same qualities: based on their handsomeness, on their ability to make women happy in bed, on their ability to amuse women and be a great company to them as "friends"? The question is posed because, for some reason, most of the women interviewees I had still wanted long-term relationships, emphasizing that satisfaction in bed will not suffice. They were interested in excellent communication, intelligence, humor, compassion, and integrity, in addition to "sexual exclusivity."

But, hey, you need to be completely naïve to think that sexual exclusivity or integrity from the side of the men can exist in our world. These "monogamy" concepts are embellished ideals created by the societies of past generations—hypocritical make-believes created so that patriarchal commitments such as marriages can live.

In our postmodern age, we can no longer trust promises and commitments from the side of men. They end up in court after just a few years of marriage for every second couple in the west. No more can we be negligent of the provisional nature of our friendships with men, to men's instability, and their inherent fickleness and playfulness, especially in today's digital age.

And, if so, why not just let them spoil us a little: Does a weekend in Paris interest you? A vacation in the Bahamas perhaps? A trendy jazz club? Quality red wine after a tasty meal? Or just an excellent Sushi with great caviar topping? Why not just let them amuse us? Challenge them a little bit. Make them think of classy entrainment before sex. Why not a spectacular opera show? A symphonic orchestra? Or an out of this world ballet?

Affection and affinity certainly exist in our world when we make up our decisions about our male "friends," but beyond "friendliness," let's not forget men's real nature and men interests before and after sex.

5

The Conquest of Female Sex

THE DOUBLE STANDARD

A friend of mine, Julie, a single thirty-one year old fashion designer from lower Manhattan, recently asked me why in my view is there still such a huge double standard when it comes to women's sexuality compared to the sexuality of men. Why in the world should an attractive young woman looking for a relationship in our modern world be degraded to the level of "whore" while in the process of dating guys? Let's be more specific for a moment and ask—why is it that a woman like Julie who dates guys for just a few dates, only to realize later they are not her cup of tea, is constantly judged by our society for being overly promiscuous?

Here is Julie's approach: She used to see the guy for a couple of dates, perhaps sleep with him, perhaps not, then, if the relationship did not take hold, at least not as she expected, she started seeing other guys, to pursue her dream of "a lover and a friend" in one man.

Regardless of if a "lover" and a "friend" could ever reside in one man—the heart of the matter is how her family reacted to her relationships with all her men. Her folks did not regard her "over fastidious experimentation" with men in a favorable light. And this for sure is an understatement. Her mother actually thought she was not so much "picky" in her approach, but, for the most part, unrespectable and degrading herself as a woman.

Amazingly, liberal Julie Thompson came from a pretty conservative U.S. family that adhered solemnly to the patriarchal familial standards, the traditional marital norms, and the interest-driven social mores associated with marriage. Her family thought that thirty-one was exactly the right time for Julie to wed. They knew she was attractive and dated a lot of guys, so they assumed there would be no problem in picking one. They were more concerned about their reputation: what other people would think and say and how they would react to Julie's proceedings with men. They did not really care what Julie felt about the men she dated and ignored the fact that Julie hadn't found her prince charming. Instead, they focused blindly on her "instability" in relationships, her "indecisiveness," and her "shameful behavior" with men.

But here is where the double standard lies: A man in the same situation of dating girls and having plenty of them would most likely be treated completely in the reverse manner. He would not be scrutinized, disparaged, scorned for seeing women and having as much sex as he wants, not even for dating multiple women in parallel. Nor would he be forced to get married at the "geriatric" age of thirty-one. Rather, such a guy will be praised and glorified by all his male friends, who were informed in advance through Facebook and Twitter about his heroic conquests in bed with all those pretty chicks. Such a guy will be admired by his friends for his working tactics to get women laid before reaching the fourth date. He will most likely become a role model for guys whose machismo is in an "inverse" correlation with the number of girls they actually get laid and the frequency they do so.

No matter how old the guy is, where he comes from, what his job is, whether he's rich or poor, black or white—our society still expects men to have plenty of sex and accepts their promiscuous behavior as a normal rule, not only when they are single but also when they are within commitments. Our society actually admires promiscuous behavior in men! It salutes them, worships them, and compliments them daily through a variety of social symbols and media channels. But when it comes to similar behavior from the side of women, even the most moderate experimentation with sex automatically invites the label of "whore."

Even within stable relationships, within the borders of family and marriage—sexual exclusivity, it appears, is perceived to be much more a woman's thing than a man's, at least in the minds of too many men in our patriarchal society. Even though monogamy is the ruling arrangement for sexual relationships today—men's double crossing is still treated forgivingly, while similar behavior from women automatically triggers penetrating criticism from the chauvinistic environment.

Unfortunately, this is the bare truth. Despite our society's great achievements in science, technology, healthcare, welfare, culture, and also in women's rights—there is still a gigantic dichotomy concerning the perception of sexual behavior of men compared with that of women. While men are expected to engage in sexual activity, preferably with various partners, both while in a relationship and while not in one—women are expected to be sin-free "Virgin Marys," committed to one single man. The patriarchal society still expects the woman to serve one man sexually, stay "pure" day and night, and look forward to putting the man's dirty linen in the laundry and taking them back—notwithstanding his occasional flings.

In this regard, adulterous men who happen to be in stable relationships behave themselves like other monogamous male species in the animal world (swans, for instance) that, alongside their existing pair bonds, enjoy occasional sex with other females, on the side.

Of course, men would rather be totally polygamous, like the Orangutans in jungles, copulating with as many females as they like—but this option was eliminated for them by the society that, for better or worse, urges that they abide by monogamy. Having no other choice, men engage themselves in "extra pair copulations" while in relationships. And when it comes to single men, they can go completely polygamous about sex if they like.

Apparently, promiscuity is an indispensable quality of being a "man." It is inescapable. It is probably coded in their genes, and it is dictating their actions day and night. For men, sex is like a drug. When under its influence, all their "engineering" goes wild and their data flows in the reverse order: from "bottom up" rather than from "top down."

Yes, men are totally controlled from below. And particularly for this reason, the patriarchal society accepted male promiscuity as part of the standard norm, while treating women's sexual activities, occasionally with the same "promiscuous" men, offensively.

The patriarchal society clearly accepts promiscuity in men to keep the male rulers sexually satisfied and intentionally rewards men for their promiscuity through a variety of social messages and positive cultural trophies. Men's promiscuity is proudly shown on TV, in sexist ads, in the press, in the cinema, through messages from celebrities and various social icons who are easy to emulate, through the trendy online social networks, and the gaming industry. All these media often objectify, commercialize, and pornographize women, reducing them to nothing but sexual objects—so men get the false impression that their behavior is acceptable for the society at large. While the naked truth is that such promiscuous behavior in men and cheap representations of women bring much harm to society. Today, women, who make up 50 percent of the world population, are victims of the overly promiscuous behavior of men.

The social hypocrisy lies in the fact that men's skirt chasing has long become the status quo, while women's experimentation with men triggers from men quite the opposite reaction: ridicule and disgust. It is not surprising, then, that year after year, national surveys conducted in the U.S. and around the western world indicate that the number of lifetime sexual partners reported by men is higher than the number of sexual partners reported by women.[1] The number of sexual partners in a lifetime reported by both genders could serve as a good measure of promiscuity for both genders. The U.S. Statistics repeatedly show that men are by far more promiscuous than women.[2] Nevertheless, it is still unclear whether the reported figures have been compromised due to social pressure. That said, it is possible that men reported an inflated number of female sexual partners to fit the "cultural expectation" from men, while women reported fewer sexual partners than they actually had due to the "whore" stigma.

Apparently, due to the old-fashioned "whore" stigma created by men centuries back, some women are still not free enough to experiment sexually in the same way that men do. Some of them cannot even get close to men's mastery level. This is because whenever such women insist on sexual freedom, they are shunned by their social circles, where women are still expected to be subservient to men. Such puritanical communities occasionally pronounce the women's verdict without conducting the trial, as if such "promiscuous" women were criminals. In the same manner, some patriarchal communities pressure women to explain their sexual activities with men and make them apologize for their "sins."

Baseless rationalizations, concocted stories, and unverified theories can be used by the hypocritical society to explain why promiscuity is happening to women today. For example, some may say, "She is overly promiscuous because she is mentally weak or emotionally unstable." Others might say, "She is overly promiscuous because of her bad education or poor upbringing at home." Still others would blame the secularist way of life with its "loose morality and broken ethics." Or, promiscuity might be attributed to women with an excess of power after women have gained their equal rights. Some misogynists, like Sigmund Freud, might use a more "scientific" explanations. They can say that it has to do with an "oral fixation" in some early psychosexual stage.

But these are all full cock-and-bull stories. Such insights are completely ungrounded on scientific evidence and are the results of the same double-faced patriarchal "truths" that make people think that experimenting with sex is a privilege of men, while committing to marriage is an obligation of women.

THE VIRGINS & THE WHORES

Amazingly, the American and the western patriarchal society still leads women by the nose, making them think they need only one partner for life. This society makes women feel they need to follow the American dream of family, home, and success.

But the reality is that the concept of marriage, an essential part of this dream, has been dead in the water, at least from the 1960s, since women became fully independent of men. No longer do women need men to lead their way and dictate to them what to do and how to do it. Women's education, suffrage, equal rights before the law, and their increasing involvement in social spheres have changed women's mindsets. The new liberties women grasped since the 1960s also prompted a metamorphosis in women's sexuality and the decisions they make about their body, about sex, and about their relationships and friendships. No longer are women naïve, weak, or modest as they were supposed to be in the past generations. And no longer are they epitomes of subservient conformity as well.

In our postmodern age, women have the intellectual means and access to information to easily discern the double standards originated by men, who still may want to subject women to their authority. Postmodern women should be able to discern a pattern of discrimination in the perception of sexual behavior of women against such behavior of men.

Society's delusive relation to marriage is a product of men's manipulations. Women today should be smart enough to understand the over tendentiousness of the patriarchal institution that presents marriage as the ultimate goal. It might be the ultimate goal, but clearly, a goal of the social institution of marriage; an institution regulated by the state and manipulated by various organizations and corporations in the free market. Such institutions, organizations, and corporations are commonly directed by men in power whose incorrigible urge to seize authority and control society makes them dictate to women what to do in various spheres: in sexuality related matters, in relationships, and marriages, fertility, kids' issues, in addition to education, career, economy, politics, and virtually every realm.

Apparently, the patriarchal society is still interested in taking advantage of women's caretaking abilities, stressing their traditional roles as wives, mothers, and maids—alongside their relatively new roles as equal breadwinners. In this regard, the participation of women in the workforce did not squelch the patriarchal trend. On the contrary, the patriarchs are now pleased to take advantage of women on the home front as well as on the job front. The patriarchal institutions still have great interest in keeping the women watchdogs of the family hearth, while at the same time they, unofficially and off the record—through legitimizing men's sexist behavior in the culture, set themselves free to experiment with sex whenever and wherever they want.

Way more than women, men often do it in existing monogamous relationships, through "extra pair copulations," no matter if they are married or not. It seems that the patriarchal society controlled by manipulative men wants to have the cake and eat it too. On the one hand, they want their women to take care of their family, kids, and homes and stay clear of any other men that might be sexually interested in them. On the other hand, they do not refrain from cheating on their women whenever and wherever they can.

While men flaunt their infidelity and embrace their promiscuity as a standard behavior, women with equal sexual desires, are viewed as nothing but dirty and disposable objects.

But why did it happen? Why did men claim a monopoly on sex? The answer is power. Men still control the world to a greater extent than women, and they would like it to remain this way. Instead, more and more women today are breaking the glass ceiling and nearing men's decision making echelons in politics, in law, in academia, in science and technology, in the arts, and within various organizations and privately held corporations—to men's great dismay.

Women would rather play with men on equal levels: at work, at home, and also in sex, but men's interests are different. Men want the power in their own hands and so they make sex and sexually related matters their own prerogative.

Men don't need women to compete on the limited resources in society which they consider theirs. So to achieve power and preserve it, men do just about everything to decrease competition from the side of women on the same resources and power channels in society: in politics and decision making, in the economy, in culture, in media, in science and technology, in education, and in entertainment. They also fight to preserve their predominance at home as prime decision makers and their lucrative positions within public institutions and corporations.

The patriarchal society communicates to women time and again that they should stick to only one man in straight monogamy and opt for patriarchal marriage. While the same patriarchal society communicates to men vicariously, though cultural symbols, that they are entitled to engage in sex as much as they want. Through such double-faced morality, the patriarchal society legitimizes sex as a male domain.

When women are not monogamous in sex or opt to experiment like men, the patriarchal society communicates to them right away they are nothing but dirty whores. It continues through objectifying women sexually and pornographizing them through the various media, using female sex for marketing various products and services. The patriarchal message is clear: men should take over sex, and the female sex should necessarily be a male's property. Women should back off, then, and let men take it all.

Through holding their reigns over the female body and the female sexuality, men's oppressive and exploitative roles linger on. They continue subjecting women to their own authority both in bed, in decision making at home, in influential positions at work, and in society at large. And they achieve that by killing two birds, by depressing women's choices about their sexuality, fertility, relationships and marriage matters, and by objectifying the female body and commercializing women sex.

Here is how it works for men: The masculine society continually restricts women’s choices about their own relationships and sexuality by using the "virgin whore" dichotomy.

According to this sexist theory, originally put in place by Sigmund Freud[3]—in the minds of men there can be two legitimate roles for the women to fit in: Either the role of a virgin (or Madonna)—reserved for the pure, loyal, and obedient woman, a wife and mother, who should not necessarily be sexually attractive to the man; or the role of a whore—reserved for the sexually appealing slutty bitch whose prime role is to be hot. And by no means can these imaginary roles overlap in the men's psyche.

This theory surmises that men can "love" their women only when they stick to the "virgin" role, as obedient wives, excellent mothers, and diligent housewives—but, unfortunately, can't get turned on by their "virgins" sexually, because they remind them of their care-giving moms. On the other hand, men can be turned on momentarily by these sexy sluts, who are ready to have sex with them at any time. The big "plus" of this theory, though, is that men can't get emotionally attached to those sluts... This conflict is at the heart of this imaginary "virgin whore dichotomy" that shockingly holds for part of our society even today. Typically, it is used by the commanding men to explain their uncontrollable pursuit of sex and their frequent infidelities. But, at the end of the day, this essentially misogynist theory allows men to justify and rationalize their cheating habits and legitimize their control of women's sexuality.

But, guess what? Sex is not a male domain, nor should it be. Especially not because of some crazy complex in men's psycho-sexual development inherited from their childhood. Despite the long lasting brainwashing throughout the entire human history, women should not believe those fictional stories. They were created artificially by power thirsty men. No matter how prevalent such justifications are, women should feel free to make their own choices about their sexuality and relationship matters exactly like men. Women can enjoy pleasurable recreational sex and celebrate it happily with long or short term partners if they like, as long as they avoid unnecessary risk. Women are sexual creatures as much as men and can have men on the side, if they want. But usually flings are excellent red lights for the women to reevaluate their existing relationships with their "stable" men.

Women should be absolutely free to become straight, lesbians, bi-sexual, single forever—whatever they feel like or makes them smile. They can cohabitate with men or live apart, start up families, raise kids if they want, be mothers, or adopt children—for patriarchal family is certainly not a must today. Women should always be free to select for themselves their golden paths in life. And in no case should they succumb to the social pressure put on them to start up monogamous, nuclear, heterosexual, and patriarchal families.

There is nothing worse than doing a thing the society tells you to do without wanting it from the bottom of your heart, even if you are thirty-seven. For instance, if you follow the marriage rule blindly, chances are you will end up stuck.

Marriage is a huge mistake when it comes to committing to a guy ready to sign the marriage contract "to love and cherish you forever"—essentially because it's a lie. No contract can guarantee the "love" of a man even for three days from signature. In all probability, the "love story" will end after a couple of years, leaving the woman with pain. Men are doomed to fail to comply with their promises regarding sex and long-term relationships because of the way their "polygamy-mindedness" was "imprinted" in their

DNAs. From the huge divorce rates today, we can learn that the marriage contract is not an exception to that. No marriage paper can really bind a woman to a man for life, no matter what the "virgin-whore" society will say.

Despite the success of women's liberation, parts of society today or, better put, the "virgin whore" parts of society, are still interested in restricting women's individual choices about sexuality, relationships, marriages, and family matters and replacing them with their own decisions. This prejudiced society wants to dictate to women how their sex lives, friendships, relationships, and, above all, marriages should look like.

The patriarchs of this society are interested in governing, controlling, and regulating decisions in order to assign to women more of the "virgin" roles, of the lovely wives and mothers, while keeping the "whores" for the men outside of the home. This, they believe, should boost their virility, both professionally and socially—taking firmer grasps on lucrative positions spearheading society (jobs that could have been taken by the "virgins" instead, but the virgins are too busy juggling home and work, ultimately compromising their advancement at work), but also sexually—through spreading their genes to the next generations.

Men just love to subject women to their authority in all aspects of their lives, in bed, at home, and at work. They want obedient virgins at home but dirty sluts outside of it. Since it guarantees their monopoly, the patriarchal leaders of society will do just everything to impose these two roles on women. And they go about it cunningly:

On the one hand, they repress women's free choices about their sex lives, sexual related matters, and relationship issues while lowering them to the level of "whores" if they don't fully comply with the "virgin" roles.

On the other hand, they commodify women's bodies and commercialize female sexuality with every service or product they sell. Doing so they provoke the "whore" image, which allows men to dream about sex all the time and also, at times, to make this dream a reality.

THOSE WOMEN WHO SELL

Sexual objectification of the female body is yet another demonic tactic used by men agenda-setters in order to control women's sexuality and sustain a social preeminence. Through showing the female body with almost every product and service they sell, various organization and privately held corporations increase their revenues in large scales.

The problem is that in our capitalistic society, female sexuality not only sells things, it also evolved into a gigantic industry generating billions of dollars in profit each year. Men of power who usually stand at the top of the popular mass media, the Internet, the press, the T.V. the film industry, and the advertizing world in corporations and conglomerates—recruit beautiful young women for various over-sexualized roles in commercials, movies, online and printed ads, and the like, to be presenters of products or services they sell.

The models' roles are pretty limited. They end up standing next to products or, better, lying idly close to them with a stupid smile on their face. But along with the discussed products or services, these young women proudly exhibit something else. Rather than their sharp brains, they showcase their feminine assets: their Donald Duck lips, their Rocky Mountains breasts, and their Candy Apple rears. Clearly, the women serve as eye candy for the horny males interested in the product or the service.

No matter if the product is material, sold out through ads, a virtual product like the TV ratings, or just a trailer for the movie theater—women's bodies are harnessed for the sale in the raunchiest way. The woman's body is used for promoting sales, speeding up monetary transactions, and closing deals. Since the capitalistic market itself is not free from patriarchal power—men were quick to capitalize on female sexuality in the ugliest way. After making female sexuality their own property, men went on and turned the objectification of women into a profession, into an industry of "glamour and success."

The main role of these young models working in the "challenging niche" of modeling or in the showbiz world is to spray sex. They are given full instructions on what to do with their bodies in order to seduce men and make them pay. When these girls are lucky enough, sometimes they can be seen "in action," using the products, or perhaps talking about the services they sell. On the face of it, those smiling faces and moving rears communicate "buy this product or service from me," but, within males' minds, they quickly translate into "come have sex with me." Captivated by the illusion of the "glamour industries," the money, and the fame—these young women fully play in men's hands. They execute the patriarchal orders precisely and in the most vulgar way. Through moving their legs, their arms, their tongues in the way that men instruct them, all they trigger is further sexist and dirty behaviors from men.

But unlike in street prostitution, most women who pose for such roles in ads do it on their own will, for usually they are paid well. And since the money is a powerful temptation, more and more young women are willing to fall into this honey trap every day. But are these young women aware of the underlying chauvinistic ideologies of such fictitious glitz and glamour scenes? Do they have an idea what patriarchal mindsets they conceal? These young slaves to capitalistic catwalks probably won't ask why they're depicted like sexual objects. Even if tyrannical obsession with power, aggression, and exploitation against women are the drive, these women are too busy and, in many cases, too doped[4] to change their attitudes.

But fact is that the sleazy objectification of women is intentional. Men have created this image to make women fit within the sexist role of the "whore" and serve as a role model for other "whores" in society. This, they believe, should strengthen the patriarchal position of men as conquerors of sex, women, society, culture, and lands. And so, whether they are aware of it or not, most women who play the objectified roles are nothing but victims of men's manipulations.

Look how stupid most women models end up looking in all those sexist ads. In most cases, their sexy looks have nothing to do with the products or the services they sell. With all due respect, there is really no connection between an almost topless model wearing a miniskirt, garters, and over the knee leather boots and hydraulic chairs or state of the art kitchens. And there is really no reason why a scantily clad teenager should ride a monstrous motorcycle, legs spread while she is selling, well... a high-speed Internet service. You are not a Mother Teresa and you needn't be one to smell the scent of prostitution in such footage. There is really no reason why the female body should be exploited and exposed to the public in this humiliating fashion. In no case is this model, and other girls like her, representatives of the companies or experts in the products or the services they promote. They have been hired to seduce men sexually, to please them visually and virtually, and make it a hard sell.

And so to achieve a sale in a capitalistic world, women's bodies are commonly marketed in the most vulgar way, along with the product or the service. It could have looked a bit better had the advertised products been related to the models in some way. For instance, if it was women's lingerie for the Victoria Secret chain these models were posing for, fewer eyebrows would be raised. But since they sell things totally unrelated to their bodies, all the women who participate in such ads should be blamed. They should be equally blamed for giving up on their freedom and sexual choices and entrusting them to men. They may not be prostitutes by profession, but they certainly do take part in this sexist prostitution trend.

Of course, this trend is part of a larger vulgar masculine culture created by men, a culture whose mission it is to get women's image and reputation stained in order to achieve male supremacy. Bottom line: The patriarchs will do everything to propagate the virgin-whore dichotomy exactly as they planned.

Evidently, the women's sexual objectification trend has disastrous implications on women's image and reputation in society. Whenever women are lowered to the ranks of "whores," audiences, women, men, and children, all get the false impression that women are equal to sex and that female sexuality is for sale. This message is spread like a virus through the “glamorous” role models, who are in most cases too young to accept the consequences for their own actions.

Again, such messages were masterfully manufactured by men who want to satisfy their appetites for sex, on the one hand; and secure for themselves familial, social, and political predominance, on the other. The "patriarchal capitalists" of society who for the most part belong to the showbiz world, to the beauty, fashion, TV, radio, advertisement, gaming, and the film industries are responsible for creating this over sexualized and demeaning climate. It is a gross climate where women's liberties to make their own choices about their bodies are traded for money. A climate where women's bodies are commodified and women are dehumanized as individuals in the ugliest way.

Now taking the notion of sexual objectification a step forward: Since the women's over sexualized body is believed to be "owned" by men, aren't men entitled to do what they want with this body? If the female's body is men's property, why can't men just use, reuse, or abuse it without women's permission? Or exploit it as they want and throw it away? Or maybe pander sex, buy and sell, import and export, make their fortunes on it? Men can, and some men do, albeit with reservations and with legal restraint.

While prostitution is illegal in most western countries and in the U.S. (excluding Nevada where the purchase and sale of sex is legal,[5] the porn industry that often spreads similar demeaning messages about women and similar sleazy pictures— lives very well.

Clearly, violent acts, abuse, sexual assault, and sexual harassment against innocent women, which are commonly seen in the prostitution and the porn worlds—exist in the real world, as well.

In extreme cases, we hear about men physically and emotionally abusing women—cursing, spitting, hitting and humiliating them. Criminal records of pathologically violent aggressors point at much harder accusations—of rape, torture, and murder. Statistics indicate that in the Western world, women are still more likely to be murdered by their intimate partners than the other way around, regardless of who started the fight.[6] A pattern of hostility against women and joy in inflicting pain in women is associated with such monstrous behaviors. While the social climate of sexual objectification which demeans the women and reduces them to nothing but whores cannot justify such vicious criminal acts and cannot relieve the sex criminals of responsibility for the crimes—the sexual objectification climate has an encouraging effect on emotionally sick, troubled, and frustrated men who are capable of cruel violence against women in the first place.

The Masters & The Slaves

Evidently, the objectification of the female body, a method used by the patriarchal capitalists of the fashion, the beauty, and the media worlds is not so easy to erase. This commodification of female sexuality is influenced and thrust forward by the mega billion dollar money spinner, the pornography industry.

The porn industry has been active as an independent player ever since the Victorian age; and although erotic depictions are as old as mankind, they have reached the masses with the development of the print industry.[7] During the nineteenth century, pornography production, its dissemination, and consumption were outlawed—yet it was still available to the nobility and the upper class scholars whose minds "could not be depraved, corrupted, or susceptible to immorality" like the minds of the masses (in the English "Obscene Publication Act" of 1857).[8] Similarly, in the U.S., pornography has been regulated, and still is today, for its materials can violate obscenity statutes if they are targeted at "prurient interests," are offensive to the "average person," or lack "serious literary, artistic, political, or scientific value" as established in Miller v. California case of 1973.[9]

However, in spite of the regulations surrounding the porn industry, especially with regard to depiction of children, inclusion of animals, and other perverse exhibitions, the hard core porn industry inflicted much more harm to the public perception of women than the glamour, the fashion, and showbiz industries altogether. Due to the demeaning nature of the presentation of the female body in porn—a woman's social image has been stained and become equal to a disposable object. Most hard core porn materials in magazines, films, and online websites are void of art and even eroticism. Nor do they impart any "serious literary, political, or scientific value." Conversely, such depictions present women as sheer vehicles, as passive objects, fully subservient to men's sexual whims, and disposable when men have had enough of their services.

You really needn't be Dr. Ruth to realize that most hardcore depictions, especially the cheap ones, are never reflections of refined sexual relationships among women and men, where good communication, mutual respect, and mutual pleasure are key to the success. Rather, these productions depict full-fledged sexual intercourse explicitly, rudely, zooming-in and out on jumbo male and female organs, while these organs are engaged in mechanical sex, usually without prior introduction or foreplay. When video is the medium for these, the plots are usually lame or nonexistent at all, and the sexual act has a tendency to be depicted instrumentally, mechanically, and impatiently to attain instant gratification for the men. In addition, if the participants have talked to each other before, during, or after the sexual act, you can call it a miracle. Typically, the vocabulary in hard core porn movies amounts to a few utterances such as "bitch," "slut," "f-words," "Oh, yes," and so forth coupled with the stereotypical moans.

While the verbal communication in hard core porn is almost nonexistent, the physical acts are violent and aggressive toward the women. In most cases, women are seen as pure victims of violent sex, penetrated brutally and ruthlessly by males alone or in a group. Coercive and torturing acts where the women are seen gagged, trussed, spat on, urinated on, whipped, slapped, hit and the like are also very common. But while those "porn star" women are instructed to let the men do what they want with their body and show them how much they love it—men are directed to keep pounding and pumping on and on. As the "plot" moves on, women are directed to falsely gasp and moan, fabricating their sexual joy and their orgasms. In the final acts, women are directed to complement the male "victory" over the sexual act through erotic facial gestures. And an immense appreciation to the powerful male for his triumphant ejaculation, usually displayed on the woman's face, is shown at the end.

Now, to cool down a little, let us turn to Immanuel Kant to understand the nature of this violent behavior of men. Why do they treat women as mere sexual objects? Why does sexual objectification happen in relationships at all? Kant discussed the notion of sexual objectification as "morally problematic"—as he believed it necessitates treatment of one partner of the other as mere "means."

But Kant also suggested that marriage gives spouses "lifelong possession of each other's sexual attributes."[10] In a way, that does not sit well with his notion of freedom of individuals in the world, men and women as "free and rational agents whose existence is an end in itself," as those women who are treated as mere objects cannot really function as "end in themselves" but "end to men's pleasures."[11]

While Kant's perspective about individualism is rather convincing, his permissible account of objectification in marriage disregards the tenacity of sexual objectification to reach disastrous proportions, especially in formal, extended, and unnatural relationships, such as marriages. In such a case, the men, who are already convinced of their supremacy over women, actually get a formal approval for that in the form of a marriage contract.

Indeed, mechanical and emotionless marriages can be the outcome of sexual-objectification-based relationships exemplified by hard-core porn.

Relationships where the only role of the man is to exploit the woman, and the only role of the woman is to serve the man in return; while both sides are pretending in public that their perverse relationship is the ultimate blessing to both.

According to the patriarchal mindset, the aspect of what "others"—family, friends, and the community at large—will think and say about the relationship is of crucial importance. Therefore, the hypocrisy in such sexually-objectifying relationships is especially grave. Oftentimes, it creates intolerable situations where women prefer suffering from offending, aggressive, and abusive men, both physically and emotionally, rather than splitting from them right away. Such patriarchal communities prefer living by rotten morals where the women cannot be "ends in themselves" as idealized by Kant, for their role is to be the "end of the men's pleasures and the men's interests" instead. According to them, women's part in the world amounts to being subservient, subordinate, and fully controlled by men.

Such patriarchal coercion exists in various levels, from the communities to the states. The patriarchs of society can come in various shapes and forms. Even within the porn industry itself, there are those who are depicted performing the brutal sexual acts ("the male porn stars"). There are those who lead the porn industry and make their fortunes on it (the "patriarchal capitalists," including the beauty, the fashion, and the media moguls, part of conglomerates). And those who lead society on the larger scale (the government, the states, and their authorities). They are all "variations" of the same patriarch: an exploiting, manipulative, and domineering power-figure who hides his sexist agendas and his eternal greediness from the public eye. But apparently, no camera flashes, no applauds from the crowd, and no enormous budgets succeed in covering up their underlying interests.

Through vulgar sexual objectification in the porn industry, men are usually portrayed as owners, masters, and leaders—while women are usually presented as objects, whores, and as slaves. Such a master-slave dialectic completely denies women of their basic right to be individuals with personal choices to make about their bodies, their relationships, and their sex lives.

Interestingly, the master slave idea has an antecedent in the Hegelian philosophy that, similarly to Kant's, discussed the relationships within marriage.[12] Such relationships, Hegel assumed, must show the wives as nothing but slaves to their husbands. Full submission to the husband was required, as women's social and financial identity was subsumed by the husband who held the social and the economic roles. Evidently, Hegel was a great believer in patriarchal marriage. And, like Aristotle, he believed in the marriage unit as a building block of the state.[13] According to Hegel, this "union of marriage" created an "ethical love" based on sharing and trust (as opposed to “sexual love”), where the consciousness of each individual, woman or man, were virtually dismissed for the benefit of the unit. Therefore, enslavement of the woman to the man and of the family to the state were essential elements for the human civil success, according to Hegel.

But can one speak of such total civil submission to the state in our postmodern world? Apparently, such an all-around submission to the state can quickly translate into a male tyranny, which in many ways persists today, in various patriarchal shapes and forms.

And this is taken to an extreme in hard-core porn, where male audiences are quick to consume the falsified message of male's conquest of female sexuality, and later, male supremacy in all aspects of society. Men quickly pass the pornographic messages on and on to more men like a lethal virus. And this is especially perilous, not when it's dealt by the philosophers, the intellectuals, or even the normative men, but when it comes into the hands of sick men.

The perverts who cannot distinguish fantasy from reality attempt to imitate the violent examples. Those pathological minds of the rapists and murderers or would-be rapists and murderers are clients of such obscene materials, exactly like normative men. But these pathologic aggressors are known for their ability to create their own delusionary translations to the violent treatment of women in porn. For instance, based on porn movies, they can assume that all women enjoy brutal, cruel, and violent sex; and thus all women would enjoy to be raped by men. They might go on with this sick logic and conclude that there is no problem with rape, which can be justified for its ability to please women and men.

However, porn is extremely popular among men of all socioeconomic backgrounds today. And although no clear cut correlation has been established so far to determine causation between hardcore pornography consumption and higher sexual crime rates—a reverse association has been found, pointing out that most of the already convicted rape criminals were in most cases also consumers of porn.[14]

FIGHTING BACK THROUGH SEX

How can the male supremacy message be countered through sex, then? Can women really be responsible for their sexual choices in a world where enormous sexist coercion still exists—not only in sex and its depictions, but also in other aspects of lives and culture? As long as the master-slave dialectic exists in our world, the hardcore pornographic materials should certainly be scrutinized, for their obscenity, vulgarity, violence, and humiliating portrayals of women. However, pronouncing pornography illegal would be like going back in time. Shutting down the porn market is not a feasible act, especially not in our electronic age, where the porn materials pass along through all the pipes, cracks, and holes on the web at the speed of light. Apparently, trying to go against the pornographic flow won't only appease the violent trends, but can also lead to their aggravation, and their further growth. In this constellation, the conquest of female sex by aggressive men might continue, and the sexual objectifications might even surpass the current vulgar rates.

Pornography cannot and should not be depressed. At least not in our democratic world, where the freedom of speech and the freedom of expression are fundamental human rights. Yet, the porn content providers should certainly reconsider the form of presentation to the public. The content must transform into something of more dignity, honor, and respect to women's personality, individuality, and character. It should present the women as equal sexual human beings with equal choices to make about their bodies and their sex life. This depiction should encourage women to be more responsible in their sexual relations with men and more controlling of their freedom as well.

The new depiction should benefit women in the same manner it benefits men. It must break down, once and for all, the patriarchal superiority concept that is still held by various believers in our chauvinistic world. It must annul the notion of the "whore," treating women as cheap sluts each time they assume their sexual roles, and tear into pieces the notion of the "virgin," part of the notorious virgin-whore coupling. This dichotomy was prevalent in the past generation, where brides were assumed to be virgins, and being unmarried at the age of twenty-one was akin to being a leper. But this notion cannot work and live in our postmodern world.

There is no reason why liberated women experimenting with their relationships and their sex lives should be treated as whores. Nor should marriage continue to be a strict social standard imposed on women in order to avoid the title of "whore". But rather, commitment to men, like sex, must be a free choice for the women to make. The new presentation must certainly support women's choice of sexuality instead of men's vulgarity. It must show women welcoming of sex as a pleasurable experience with men, rather than a painful struggle with men and from men.

Perhaps the best way would be to present women in full control of their sexuality. Inferiority of the female role in a sexual activity should be replaced by full equality in a pleasurable play. The hit and run bang-bang style of porn's presentations must go away. And the delicate erotic presentation should compliment both women and men and present both of them as equal individuals with similar rights and desires to enjoy one another through mutually rewarding play.

After all, both women and men are sexual creatures deserving to engage with one another in one of the most pleasurable activities endowed to human beings on earth. Women and men alike are entitled to have wonderful, healthful, and celebratory sex, when it is associated with recreation and play and not just with reproduction. It's just that the men have conquered sex from the women and made it their own prerogative, like other valuable assets, properties, lands, and rights in society. So perhaps the "slaves" and the "masters" should be replaced by both parties being the "masters." And the “whores” and the “virgins” should both fade away.

NOTES

Chapter 1

(1) Johan C. Karremans et al., "Interacting with Women Can Impair Men's Cognitive Functioning," *Journal of Experimental Social Psychology* 45, no 4 (2009): 1041-1044, https://docs.google.com/file/d/0B-5-JeCa2Z7hdDZvWURZc2dvQk0/edit?pref=2&pli=1

(2) K. Grammer and A. Jütte, "Battle of Odors: Significance of Pheromones for Human Reproduction,"*Gynakol Geburtshilfliche Rundsch* 37, no.3 (1977): 150-53.

(3) Charles R. Darwin, *On the Origin of Species by Means of Natural Selection, or the Preservation of Favoured Races in the Struggle for Life* (London: John Murray, 1859), http://darwinonline.org.uk/content/frameset?itemID=F373&viewtype=text&pageseq=1/

(4) Helen E. Fisher, Arthur Aron, and Lucy L. Brown, "The Neurobiology of Social Recognition, Attraction and Bonding," *Philosophical Transactions of the Royal Society* 361 (2006): 2173-2186, http://www.helenfisher.com/downloads/articles/Article_final_JRS_06.pdf

(5) P. Tucker and Arthur Aron, "Passionate Love and Marital Satisfaction at Key Transition Points in the Family Life Cycle," *Journal of Social and Clinical Psychology* 12, no. 2 (1993): 135–147.

(6) Beautiful Women Can Be Bad for Your Health, According to Scientists," *The Telegraph,* May 3, 2010, http://www.telegraph.co.uk/news/newstopics/howaboutthat/7668344/Beautiful-women-can-be-bad-for-your-health-according-to-scientists.html

(7) Ihab Hassan, "The Culture of Postmodernism," *Theory, Culture, and Society* 2, no. 3 (1985): 119-131.

(8) Stephanie Coontz, *Marriage, a History: From Obedience to Intimacy, or How Love Conquered Marriage* (New York: Viking Press, 2005).

(9) "Marriage and Divorce Rates by Country," *The US Census Bureau Statistical Abstract*, 2011, http://www.census.gov/compendia/statab/2011/tables/11s1335.pdf

(10) Kenneth Mah and Yitzchak M. Binik, "The Nature of Human Orgasm: a Critical Review of Major Trends". *Clinical Psychology Review* 21, no.6 (2001): 823–56.

(11) Susan M. Hughes and Daniel J. Kruger, "Sex Differences in Post-Coital Behaviors in Long and Short-Term Mating: An Evolutionary Perspective," *Journal of Sex and Research* 48, no.5 (2011): 496-505.

(12) Susan Kuchinskas, *The Chemistry of Connection: How the Oxytocin Response Can Help You Find Trust, Intimacy, and Love* (Oakland CA: New Harbinger Publications, 2009), 73-99.

(13) Mike Nichols," Adult Separation Anxiety

Disorder," *Anxiety, Panic and Health,* June 30, 2008, http://anxietypanichealth.com/reference/separation-anxiety-disorder-adult/

Chapter 2

(1) Laura K. Guerrero, Peter A. Andersen, and Walid A. Afifi, *Close encounters: Communication in Relationships* (Thousand Oaks, CA: Sage Publications, 2007).

(2) John Elliott and Rachel Dobson, "Straying wives match men as marital cheats," *The Sunday Times*, October 26, 2003, http://www.thesundaytimes.co.uk/sto/news/uk_news/article26365.ece

(3) David M. Buss and David P. Schmitt, "Sexual Strategies Theory: An Evolutionary Perspective of Human Mating," *Psychological Review* 100, no. 2 (1993): 204-232, http://www.psy.cmu.edu/~rakison/bussandschmitt.pdf

(4) David M. Buss, "Strategies of Human Mating," *Psychological Topics* 15, no. 2 (2006): 239-260.

(5) Michael J. Formica, "Gender Differences, Sexuality and Emotional Infidelity," *Psychology Today, Enlightened Living Blog,* http://www.psychologytoday.com/blog/enlightened-living/200901/gender-differences-sexuality-and-emotional-infidelity

(6) David A. DeSteno et al., "Sex Differences in

Jealousy: Evolutionary Mechanism or Artifact of Measurement?" *Journal of Personality and Social Psychology* 83, no.5 (2002): 1103-1116.

(7) "Sexual Partner Status Affects A Woman's, But Not A Man's, Interest In The Opposite Sex," *ScienceDaily,* June 3, 2009, http://www.sciencedaily.com/releases/2009/05/090528120657.htm

(8) David M. Buss and David P. Schmitt, "Sexual Strategies Theory: An Evolutionary Perspective of Human Mating," *Psychological Review* 100, no. 2 (1993): 204-232, http://www.psy.cmu.edu/~rakison/bussandschmitt.pdf

(9) Bram P. Buunk et al., "Age and Gender Differences in Mate Selection Criteria for Various Involvement Levels," *Personal Relationships* 9, no.3 (2002): 271-278.

(10) James Bennet and Jill Abramson, "Lawyers Say Tape of Clinton Shows Regret and Anger," *The New York Times,* September 20, 1998, http://www.nytimes.com/1998/09/20/us/testing-president-overview-lawyers-say-tape-clinton-shows-regret-anger.html?pagewanted=all&src=pm

(11) Peter Baker and Helen Dewar," The Senate Acquits President Clinton," *The Washington Post,* February 13, 1999, http://www.washingtonpost.com/wp-srv/politics/special/clinton/stories/impeach021399.htm

(12) John Marshall Townsend, Jeffrey Kline, and Timothy H. Wasserman, "Low-investment Copulation: Sex Differences in Motivations and Emotional Reactions," *Ethology and Sociobiology* 16, no.1 (1995): 25-51.

(13) Thomas Laqueur, *Making Sex: Body and Gender From the Greeks to Freud* (Cambridge, Harvard University Press, 1992).

(14) Chris Cillizza, "Where in the World is Mark Sanford?" *'The Fix' Blog by the Washington Post*, June 22, 2009, http://voices.washingtonpost.com/thefix/governors/where-in-the-world-is-mark-san.html?wprss=thefix

(15) Tamara Lush and Evan Berland, "AP Newsbreak: SC Gov 'Crossed Lines' with Women," *Associated Press*, Jun 30, 2009, http://www.breitbart.com/article.php?id=D9955KDG2

(16) Tonya Cunningham, "Psychological Effects of Cheating," *ehow*, December 06, 2010, http://www.ehow.co.uk/list_7608874_psychological-effects-cheating.html

(17) Saul L. Miller and Jon K. Maner," Sex Differences in Response to Sexual Versus Emotional Infidelity: The Moderating Role of Individual Differences," *Personality and Individual Differences* 46 (2009): 287–291, https://www2.psy.uq.edu.au/~uqbziets/MillerS2009_Sex_difference_in_sexual_vs_emotional%20jealousy_role_of_ind_diffs.pdf

(18) Lawrence M. Friedman, *American Law in the Twentieth Century, (*New Haven: Yale University Press, 2002), 430-55.

(19) "Divorce and Separation: an Overview," *Cornell University Law School*, August 19, 2010, http://www.law.cornell.edu/wex/divorce

(20) Susan Bayley, *"Victorian Values: An Introduction" Dawson College*, 2008, http://www.scribd.com/doc/31333018/wikipediaboek

(21) Robert W. Price, *Roadmap to Entrepreneurial Success* (New York: AMACOM, 2004), 31-49.

(22) Peggy Vaughan, *The Monogamy Myth: A Personal Handbook for Recovering from Affairs* (New York: Newmarket Press, 1998).

(23) Varleries Bauerlein and Alex Roth," Sanford Odyssey Ends in Tears," *The Wall Street Journal*, Politics, June 25, 2009, http://online.wsj.com/article/SB124584667616347147.html

(24) Bonnie Fuller," Arnold Schwarzenegger Has Triply Betrayed His Wife Maria Shriver & *All* His Kids!" *Huffington Post Entertainment*, May 17, 2011, http://www.huffingtonpost.com/bonnie-fuller/arnold-schwarzenegger-love-child_b_863175.html

(25) "Tiger Woods Voted AP Athlete of the Decade," *CBSNews*, December 17, 2009, http://www.cbsnews.com/stories/2009/12/16/sportsline

/main5986267.shtml

Chapter 3

(1) "The Tenets of Biblical Patriarchy," *Vision Forum Ministries,2011,* https://homeschoolersanonymous.files.wordpress.com/2014/04/the-tenets-of-biblical-patriarchy-vision-forum-ministries.pdf

(2) Bronislaw Malinowski, *Sex and Repression in Savage Society* (London: Routledge & Kegan Paul, 1937), http://www.archive.org/stream/sexrepressionins00mali#page/n5/mode/2up

(3) Aristotle, *Politics: A Treatise on Government,* trans. William Ellis A.M., Project Gutenberg EBook of Politics,1912, http://www.gutenberg.org/files/6762/6762-h/6762-h.htm

(4) Simone De Beauvoir, *The Second Sex, trans.* Constance Borde and Sheila Malovany-Chevallier (Vintage, 2011).

(5) Kate Thomas,"77 Cents On a Man's Dollar: Women Still Earn Less than Men," *The SEIU Blog*, April 20, 2010, http://www.seiu.org/2010/04/77-cents-on-a-mans-dollar-women-still-earn-less-than-men.php

(6) Michelle J. Budig and Paula England, "The Wage Penalty for Motherhood," *American Sociological Review* 66, no.2 (2001): 204-225, http://courses.washington.edu/pbafadv/examples/TheWagePenaltyforMotherhood.pdf

(7) Gerda Lerner, *The Creation of Patriarchy* (New York: Oxford University Press, 1987)

(8) Tamara K. Hareven, "The History of the Family and the Complexity of Social Change," *The American Historical Review* 96, no. 1 (1991): 95–124.

(9) Louis Dupre, *The Enlightenment & the Intellectual Foundations of Modern Culture* (New Haven: Yale University Press, 2005), 153-186.

(10) Richard Seel, *The Uncertain Father: Exploring Modern Fatherhood* (San Diego: Gateway, 1987).

(11) Mary Beard, *Woman as a Force in History A study in Traditions and Realities* (New York: Macmillan, 1946).

(12) Sheila Cronan, "Marriage," in *Radical Feminism*, ed. Anne Koedt, Ellen Levine, and Anita Rapone (New York: Quadrangle, 1973).

(13) Pauline Kleingeld, "Just Love? Marriage and the Question of Justice," *Social Theory and Practice* 24, no.2 (1998): 261-281.

(14) J. C. Barden, "Marital Rape: Drive for Tougher Laws is Pressed," *The New York Times*, 13 May 1987,

http://www.nytimes.com/1987/05/13/us/marital-rape-drive-for-tougher-laws-is-pressed.html

(15) Susan M. Hartmann, *The Home Front and Beyond: American Women in the 1940s* (Boston: Twayne Publishers, 1982).

(16) Stephanie Coontz, *Marriage, a History: From Obedience to Intimacy, or How Love Conquered Marriage* (New York: Viking Press, 2005).

(17) Catharine Edwards, *The Politics of Immorality in Ancient Rome* (Cambridge: Cambridge University Press, 2002).

(18) Joseph Henrich "Polygyny in Cross Cultural Perspective Theory and Implications," in Joseph Henrich Affidavit, *The Vancouver Sun*, July 15, 2010, 24-64.

(19) Ulrich H. Reichard, "Monogamy: Past and Present," in *Monogamy Mating Strategies and Partnerships in Birds, Humans and other Mammals,* eds. Ulrich H. Reichard and Christophe Boesch (Cambridge: Cambridge University Press, 2003), 3-25.

(20) George P. Murdock, "Ethnographic Atlas Codebook," *World Cultures* 10, no. 1(1998): 86-136, http://eclectic.ss.uci.edu/~drwhite/worldcul/Codebook4EthnoAtlas.pdf

(21) Farai Chideya, "The M Word: Talking Marriage and Monogamy in the Time of Tiger Woods," *The Root*, December 18, 2009,

http://www.theroot.com/views/m-word-talking-marriage-and-monogamy-time-tiger-woods

(22) Laura K. Guerrero, Peter A. Andersen, and Walid A. Afifi, *Close encounters: Communication in Relationships* (Thousand Oaks, CA: Sage Publications, 2007), 281-305.

(23) "Federal Defense of Marriage Act (DOMA)," *DOMA Watch*, Alliance Defense Fund, 2008, https://www.gpo.gov/fdsys/pkg/BILLS-104hr3396enr/pdf/BILLS-104hr3396enr.pdf

(24) Michelle Foucault, preface to *Anti-Oedipus: Capitalism and Schizophrenia, by* Gilles Deleuze and Felix Guattari, trans. Robert Hurley, Mark Seem, and Helen R. Lane (Minneapolis: Minnesota UP, 1983),iv.

(25) John Locke, *Two Treatises of Government,* ed. Peter Laslett, (Cambridge: Cambridge University Press, 1988), 265-325.

(26) John Stuart Mill, *The Subjection of Women,* ed. Susan Moller Okin (Indianapolis: Hackett Publishing Company, 1988).

(27) Friedrich Engels, *The Origin of the Family, Private Property, and the State,* ed. Eleanor Burke Leacock (New York: International Publishers, 1972), 94-146.

(28) Karl Marx, "The Communist Manifesto," in *Selected Writings*, ed. Lawrence H. Simon (Indianapolis: Hackett, 1994), 157-186.

(29) Wilhelm Reich, *The Sexual Revolution: Toward a Self-Governing Character Structure,* trans. Theodore P. Wolfe (New York: Farrar, Straus and Giroux, 1963), 71-79.

Chapter 4

(1) Carl N. Degler, *At Odds: Women and the Family in America from the Revolution to the Present* (Oxford: Oxford University Press, 1981), 178-226.

(2) Adam Smith, *The Wealth of Nations. An Inquiry Into the Nature and Causes of The Wealth of Nations* (Florida: Simon & Brown, 2011), 223-246.

(3) Thomas L. Friedman, *The World Is Flat: A Brief History of the Twenty-First Century* (New York: Farrar, Straus and Giroux, 2005).

(4) John Gowdy, *Limited Wants, Unlimited Means: A Reader on Hunter-Gatherer Economics and the Environment* (Washington D.C.: Island Press, 1998), 255-280.

(5) Richard B. Lee and Irven DeVore eds., *Man The Hunter* (New York: Aldine De Gruyter, 1999)

(6) Paul Veyne, "The Household and its Freed Slaves," in *A History of Private Life From Pagan Rome to Byzantium, eds.* Philippe Ariès and Georges Duby (Cambridge: Belknap Press, Harvard University Press, 1992), 71-94.

(7) Joseph R. Strayer, *Western Europe in the Middle Ages: A Short History* (Chicago: Waveland Press, 1991).

(8) Peter Burke, "The Spread of Italian Humanism," in *The Impact of Humanism on Western Europe*, eds. Anthony Goodman and Angus MacKay (London: Longman, 1990), 1-22.

(9) William Shakespeare, *Romeo and Juliet* (Seattle: CreateSpace, 2011).

(10) Peter Burke, *The European Renaissance: Centre and Peripheries* (Oxford: Wiley-Blackwell, 2006),101-169.

(11) Stephen Greenblatt et al. eds., *The Norton Anthology of English Literature, Volume D: The Romantic Period* (New York: W.W. Norton & Company, 2006).

(12) Ray B. Williams, "Has gender equity taken a step backwards?," *Wired For Success Blogs, Psychology Today,* March 6, 2011, http://www.psychologytoday.com/blog/wired-success/201103/has-gender-equity-taken-step-backwards

(13) Karremans et al., "Interacting with women can impair men's cognitive functioning," *Journal of Experimental Social Psychology* 45, no. 4 (2009): 1041-1044.

(14) Lindsay Shugerman, "Percentage of married

couples who cheat," *catalogs.com Info Library*, April, 2007, http://www.catalogs.com/info/relationships/percentage-of-married-couples-who-cheat-on-each-ot.html

Chapter 5

(1) Martin Beckford and Alastair Jamieson," Britain is among casual sex capitals of the Western world, research claims," *The Telegraph*, 30 Nov 2008, http://www.telegraph.co.uk/health/healthnews/3536598/Britain-is-among-casual-sex-capitals-of-the-Western-world-research-claims.html

(2) "New survey tells how much sex we're having," *msnbc.com, The Associated Press*, June 22, 2007, http://www.msnbc.msn.com/id/19374216/

(3) Sigmund Freud, "A Special Type of Object Choice Made by Men," *in The Standard Edition of the Complete Psychological Works of Sigmund Freud, Volume XI* (New York: General Books LLC, 2010), 165–175.

(4) Christopher Hope, "Models and actors are glamorising cocaine use, says George W Bush's drugs tzar," *The Telegraph*, 11 September, 2008. http://www.telegraph.co.uk/news/worldnews/northamerica/usa/2798800/Models-and-actors-are-glamorising-cocaine-use-says-George-W-Bushs-drugs-tzar.html

(5) Guy Louis Rocha, "History of Prostitution in Nevada," *Nevada State Library and Archives*, 4

August 1999, http://www.bunnyranch.com/news/history/Nevada_State_Library_and_Archives/

(6) Stacey B. Plichta, "Intimate Partner Violence and Physical Health Consequences: Policy and Practice Implications," *Journal of Interpersonal Violence* 19, no.11 (2004): 1296–1323.

(7) Harford Montgomery Hyde, *A History of Pornography* (New York: Farrar, Straus and Giroux, 1965).

(8) "The Obscene Publication Act, 1857," *BBC Edited Guide Entry*, 30th January 2002, http://www.bbc.co.uk/dna/h2g2/A679016

(9) "Miller v. California, 413 U.S. 15 (1973)," *Justia.com, US Supreme Court Center*, 2004. http://supreme.justia.com/us/413/15/case.html

(10) Immanuel Kant, *The Metaphysics of Morals*, ed. Mary J. Gregor (Cambridge: Cambridge University Press, 1996), 37-86.

(11) Catherine A. MacKinnon, *Feminism Unmodified: Discourses on Life and Law* (Cambridge, MA: Harvard University Press, 1988), 46-62.

(12) Georg Wilhelm Fredrich Hegel, *Elements of the Philosophy of Right,* ed. Allen W. Wood, *trans.* H. B. Nisbet (Cambridge: Cambridge University Press, 1995), 209-210.

(13) Aristotle, *The Complete Works of Aristotle: The Revised Oxford Translation, ed.* Jonathan Barnes (Princeton, NJ: Princeton University Press, 1984).

(14) Diana Scully, *Understanding Sexual Violence: A Study of Convicted Rapists* (New York: HarperCollins Academic, 1990), 53-57.

Made in the
USA
Monee, IL

14853912R00118